# Bringing Christ Back

# Bringing Christ Back

Restoring Christ's Powerful Presence

Harold Ewing Burchett

Bringing Christ Back Ministries
www.bcbministries.com

First edition 2006
Second edition published 2015 by
Bringing Christ Back Ministries
www.bcbministries.com

ISBN: 978-0-9898179-1-2

Cover design by Barry Durham

Printed in the United States of America

The Scripture quotations in this publication are taken from the *Holy Bible, New International Version*, copyright © 1973, 1978, 1984 by the International Bible Society. Used by permission of Zondervan Bible Publishers.

To my wife, Jane, who labored beside me for more than forty years
before being stricken with Alzheimer's disease.

And to the faithful ones in our house church,
who have continued in prayer on behalf of *Bringing Christ Back*
and who have sustained me as I have tended my ailing loved one
while writing this book.

# CONTENTS

# FIGURES

# FOREWORD

The title of this book—*Bringing Christ Back*—and the urgency of its words are reminiscent of the great English preacher John Bunyan, author of the still-popular *Pilgrim's Progress* (first published in 1678). In Bunyan's second great allegory, *The Holy War* (1682), Prince Emmanuel and his forces capture the town of Mansoul from its evil lord, Diabolus. The Prince then moves into the town, clothes each person with his distinctive white garment, and interacts intimately with all the citizens.

All is not well, however, for Mr. Carnal Security, a holdover from the previous regime, manages to beguile the citizens. He calls attention to their present strong fortifications and to the great assurances from Emmanuel that they would be happy forever. Imperceptibly, their delight in living in Emmanuel's presence starts to fade, and content in their now-strong position, they find delight in other things. The result? Emmanuel quietly leaves the city. The strong, secure, orthodox citizens, however, "were so hardened in their way, and had so drunk in the doctrine of Mr. Carnal Security, that the departing of their Prince touched them not, nor was he remembered by them when gone; and so of consequence his absence not condoled [grieved] by them."[1]

---

[1] John Bunyan, *The Holy War, Made by Shaddai upon Diabolus, for the Regaining of the Metropolis of the World,* ed. James F. Forrest (New York: New York University Press, 1968), p. 175.

Harold Burchett, for one, grieves the absence of this Prince from the church, the body of his people. He mourns the fact that the powerful presence of this Savior is all too often not a reality in the everyday lives of those who claim his salvation, or in many churches who call him their Head. Christ has withdrawn, but few seem to notice. What does it take, he asks, to actually *bring Christ back* to such lives and such churches?

If these concerns touch a nerve in your own soul, then you have picked up the right book. Read on!

Be ready, though, to take it slow, for the author covers lots of ground. He first reviews a number of "grand truths now fuzzy," then analyzes "crucial practices now weakened." For the first part, the author digs beneath a surface view of Christ, focusing especially on his incarnation, but also addressing his sinless life, his dealing with the threefold problem of human sin, his resurrection and ascension into the Father's presence, and his present actions for us. He shows how these truths, when brought into sharp focus, can transform the daily practices of every believer and mark the tone of every church.

The exposition is lively, filled with uncommon freshness of phrase. And readers will encounter several startling stories from the author's experience showing how needy men and women came to a new grasp of truth about Christ, which led in turn to remarkable personal transformations.

Throughout, the author is jealous to rescue the truths and applications surrounding the incarnation of the Son of God from well-meaning but careless preachers and writers whose words have obscured these truths and therefore blocked the transformations that they are meant to produce. Again, be ready to take it slow. Plan to read the book a second time. Weigh the arguments carefully. Examine each truth expectantly, as you would a missing coin purse just rediscovered.

My wife and I first met Harold Burchett in October 1973. Then in December 1974 we moved from the Midwest to join his church in New England, where he was our pastor for five years. We saw firsthand the power of truth to transform lives. Pastor Burchett moved on to other pastorates and other responsibilities, but to this day, people continue to be deeply touched by his personal teaching and counseling. Over the years I have edited several of Harold's books, including this one, the most comprehensive yet.[2]

From 1985 to the present, I have worked full-time as academic editor—free-lance for ten years and then, since 1995, for the William B. Eerdmans Publishing Company, Grand Rapids, Michigan. In all these years I have edited books and articles of about 1,500 authors, of all nationalities, all faiths. None of this writing, however, has had the effect on my heart the following brief paragraph did from the preface of the book you are holding:

> Familiar doctrinal phrasing may be recited long after the words themselves have lost any meaning or vitality. Jesus not only promised the Spirit of truth to help us "get it right," but he added these words concerning the obedient disciple: "I too will love him and *show myself* to him" (John 14:21). Truth that is clear and the presence of Christ that is real—these two are forever bound together.

Even as a child, I knew all about Jesus the Christ and about

---

[2] Previous editing projects for Harold Burchett have been *Spiritual Life Studies: A Manual for Personal Edification* (1980) and *Healing for the Church: New Life for You and Your Church* (1989), both published by the author, and *Last Light: Staying True through the Darkness of Alzheimer's* (NavPress, 2002).

his sending the Spirit. But as a professional editor helping a friend prepare his book-of-a-lifetime, when I came to this paragraph I somehow instantly knew that I had not been seeing much of what Jesus had to show me personally, that for me the reality of this divine presence was pitifully thin. I took a second look, then, at the "truth that is clear" that was supposedly bound together with the presence of Christ. Not as clear as I thought it was! I was more than ready, then, to work at scratching off the fuzz from the grand truths covered in part 1 and to take a concerned look at the crucial practices reviewed in part 2.

Working through this text, then, as both editor and reader, has proved to be unusually fruitful for me, stirring a new love for both the old truth and the present reality of Christ. I would like to think that even my marriage and my church have seen something new in the bargain. Others, though, will have to tell those stories.

Read on, I say, with mind open and heart ready for something old-but-new!

CRAIG A. NOLL
Editor, Wm. B. Eerdmans Publishing Co.

# PREFACE

More than seventy years have passed since I began my Christian journey. But time in service does not by itself bring knowledge of the Holy God. To know truly about God, one must know what is unknowable, except for revelation from God.

Then, according to Jesus, only "little children" are brought into this truth. Much of it is hidden from those who are "wise and learned." Our understanding of God and his things is limited, shaped, or misshaped by our inner condition. Big truth is for little people, according to Jesus (Luke 10:21).

No one enters God's family and lives close up with him by knowing everything. One day we shall understand things more fully, but for now, we may be saved and have new life in Christ when we repent and surrender to the essential truth that we do possess about Jesus Christ as Lord and Savior. We come to know all that this truth means as we grow. The key to this knowing is repentance and humble submission to truth. Then we are assured by 1 John 3:24, "Those who obey his commands live in him, and he in them. And this is how we know that he lives in us: We know it by the Spirit he gave us."

Failure to continue in this early posture of humble dependence causes a distancing from God. Furthermore, if those who handle the truth as teachers and guides become lax themselves, the Spirit of truth is grieved, and Christ withdraws. Practice may continue, but power will be missing.

Familiar doctrinal phrasing may be recited long after the words themselves have lost any meaning or vitality. Jesus not only promised the Spirit of truth to help us "get it right," but he added these words concerning the obedient disciple: "I too will love him and show myself to him" (John 14:21). Truth that is clear and the presence of Christ that is real—these two are forever bound together.

We who are conservative "Bible believers" are generally agreed on which major doctrinal points we subscribe to. Underneath the formulations, however, are critical variations in our understanding of those doctrines and often a carelessness in defining them.

Since God's ways and thoughts are so far above ours (Isa. 55:9), we are totally dependent on the mercy of his revelation in Scripture. "The secret things belong to the Lord our God, but the things revealed belong to us and to our children forever, that we may follow all the words of this law" (Deut. 29:29).

Revealed truth is ours to be sought out and understood. To lag and fail in this pursuit is to grieve our Lord and cause a withdrawal on his part, perhaps unnoticed by us. Tarnished truth will do little to warn adherents that our Lord is missing.

The writing that follows is presented in two parts. Part 1, "Grand Truths Now Fuzzy," intends to show that some of our most valuable and essential truths have been allowed to slip from our clear understanding. This laxness is a grief to our Lord, whose wounding is taking place primarily in the "house of his friends" (see Zech. 13:6).

Part 2, "Crucial Practices Now Weakened," aims at showing that the dimming of light detailed in part 1 has inevitable consequences in our praying, our teaching and preaching, our counseling, the effectiveness of our war against Satan, and our understanding of the church and our practice of church life.

Such an approach will, I hope, demonstrate that struggling to fix problems of part 2 is futile until matters of part 1 are put right. This needed restoration will first require a deep repentance and a deliberate choice to bring back the King to his rightful place.

# INTRODUCTION

Something that is both lost and thought to be safe is doubly lost. When the hidden is thought to be in hand, it will not be sought. Anxious children frequently check to make certain their parents are still at home, in the house. Let us now make that search for evidence of our Lord's vital presence among us.

What if we should claim to "have Jesus" when, in actual fact, there existed little evidence of his presence in us and about us? Would that not indeed be a mistaken, even arrogant, presumption? As we make our investigation of this very matter, remember that familiar phrases, often repeated without depth of meaning, tend to shut down mind and heart. Nobody will ask, "What *really* is wrong?" "Where *is* Jesus?"

Strangely enough, the teachers mentioning most often that Jesus is missing are those liberal in theology. They endlessly discuss their pilgrimage to discover the true Christ of history while subjecting the gospel accounts to dismemberment by scalpels of intellectualism.

But a certain fuzziness held in a mechanical, determined grip seems to mark and mar many who call themselves Bible believers. Shadows fall over Jesus, for the real Jesus is not like the one some presume to worship and proclaim. These people "take their stand" and argue their case, but clear truth does not long live, and certainly shows little power, where there is only empty repetition of familiar phrasing about our Lord's person and work.

Teachings of cults are tested and exposed using this double touchstone of the person and work of our Lord. Both must be square. Good. But what of those who proclaim both these areas of truth in proper, traditional words that fall short of conveying much vital truth? What if the "solid" sermons have allowed a gradual drift into a shadowed falseness? No alarms are sounded, but things are not right.

## What Is Promised and What Is Possessed
Promises that are preached but not really possessed can be hurtful. Jesus withdraws, hides. While his coming might be announced, his going might not be.

Scripture says of our era, "A better hope is introduced, by which we draw near to God" (Heb. 7:19). And again, "No matter how many promises God has made, they are 'Yes' in Christ" (2 Cor. 1:20). We are invited to experience a life close-up with God. As Christ profoundly stresses in John 14–16, he is sending the Holy Spirit to us so that "on that day you will realize that I am in my Father, and you are in me, and I am in you. . . . He who loves me will be loved by my Father, and I too will love him and show myself to him" (14:20-21).

Our Lord goes on to explain that this new intimacy with him will be sustained by personal instruction from the Spirit of truth and a new alignment in prayer between the believer and God, using Christ's name. The wonder of this relationship is almost beyond words, but to let it slide or fade amounts to a tragedy beyond words. Are you, am I, what Christ died and rose to produce?

## How Things Are and How Things Ought to Be
All our advanced modern methods in marketing the Christian message cannot hide the unsettling fact that the personal presence

2

of the Lord Jesus seems not powerfully evident in many lives and churches. Even our hope of Christ's second coming must not make us neglectful of our "now" blessings, offered to us in Scripture. To the blinded, lackadaisical church of Laodicea Jesus gave a direct rebuke and then a promise, filled with insight for our study here: "Be earnest, and repent. Here I am! I stand at the door and knock. If anyone hears my voice and opens the door, I will come in and eat with him, and he with me" (Rev. 3:19-20).

Looking for Jesus to return a second time while forcing him to knock for entrance now is a remarkably strange situation. How did we get where we are today? Exactly where are we?

Our plight might be put this way: We have lost content from our bottles of truth, but we have faithfully tended and protected their labels. These accepted, no-thought-necessary stickers carry familiar wording, and in some cases they are burnished with stylish logos and the latest seminar buzzwords. Even things true, however, lose strength of impact when held in hands calloused by familiarity. Mere labels, traded like collectables, have usurped the place once held by thought-out truth. Phrases like "the finished work" (of Christ) or "positional truth" no longer leap with life. They languish among the heap of barely breathing "sleeper terms," allowing escape from doing much thinking. When such terms are not clearly defined, they become like so much in-house jargon, permitting the precious to become hackneyed.

Showing Christ to a world that won't look is a large challenge! Fortunately, God in scriptural revelation puts great spiritual truth in understandable terms—even putting teachings about himself in the bottom drawer, where little ones can reach them. He is neither dishonored nor obscured by simple expression. The very point of revelation is to make things reachable that are beyond us. Our problem, then, is not that the Bible is so difficult but that we have allowed core truths to get so out of focus that we can't see what God has put there for us to see. Together, let's take a fresh look at what God has spread before us.

## One Word Summarizes the Entire Scripture: "Christ"

"The Scriptures . . . testify about me," said Jesus in John 5:39, and in verse 46, "If you believed Moses, you would believe me, for he wrote about me." Then, so that none might miss the fact that he is the Grand Center of all Scripture, the Lord later taught his disciples, "Everything must be fulfilled that is written about me in the Law of Moses, the Prophets and the Psalms." He then "opened their minds so that they could understand the Scriptures," telling them, "This is what is written: The Christ will suffer and rise from the dead on the third day, and repentance and forgiveness of sins will be preached in his name to all nations, beginning at Jerusalem" (Luke 24:44-47).

The apostle Paul wrote of his struggle for the believers of Laodicea and Colosse "that they may know the mystery of God, namely, Christ, in whom are hidden all the treasures of wisdom and knowledge" (Col. 2:2-3). Getting to God and knowing him is altogether and only through Jesus Christ. Miss the door and you don't get in, not even if you are very close.

Before this magnificence, we stand like a bewildered man peering through the window of his snow-covered and locked car. There are his keys in the ignition. Everything in the car is close, familiar, once held in hand, yet now it is beyond reach because of thoughtlessness.

Consider further this analogy. Keys are devices for unlocking doors. Doors are devices for getting through walls. Walls are devices that separate what is within from what is without. With no key, the locked door becomes a part of the wall. When Jesus teaches us that he is the door, he is plainly admitting that the wall is there. He is making it clear, though, that he is not part of the wall but is the way through it. And since he is the door, we are encouraged to lay hold of those key truths about our Lord that open to us vast realms of knowledge.

## What Is Lost and What Is Left

The powerful presence of our enemy, the god of this world, is overwhelmingly evident in his vast arena: the whole social and cultural world, with its crass immorality, greed and materialism, violence, godless philosophies, and crime, both organized and personal. In the face of this well-entrenched, godless system, is Jesus Christ powerfully present with his people? Perhaps we make commendable efforts to get the manger scene back in the town square or to preserve the phrase "in God we trust" on our money—but *where is Jesus?* Where is the evidence *in our world* of his kingship? Are we "strong in the Lord and in his mighty power" (Eph. 6:10)? No, instead of a powerful Presence, there is too often only an ominous absence, a disquieting quiet.

Revering the empty bottles that once held precious truth is somewhat like the Israelites continuing to worship the once-effective bronze serpent. The serpent was originally appointed by God in Numbers 21:4-9 but was foolishly venerated until Hezekiah's day (2 Kings 18:4). Perhaps Jonah's pitiable cry is apropos for our day: "Those who cling to worthless idols forfeit the grace that could be theirs" (Jonah 2:8). What could be, is not ours—not really.

Keep firmly in mind that dark reigns only where light is not. Where Jesus resides with warm welcome, he rules and stands with his people against opposition. We thus have come to our key question: Where is Jesus? We must not be surprised that the sinful world is indeed sinful and hates light. Our concern, rather, must be to discover the obstructions within the heart and understanding of church people that veil, hide, grieve, and turn away our Lord.

Before we begin our search, let me reiterate that keeping a sound statement of Christology in our system of theology is not enough, as we shall soon see. Furthermore, venturing to make a casual or disinterested dissection of things infinite and almighty can be deadening, if not deadly. It is to be hoped that we can reach our goal without falling into these traps.

## Getting Started—Simply

"But as for me, it is good to be near God" (Ps. 73:28). We *can* know God, and we *can* be near God. The great news is that there is a bridge that spans the gulf between God and us. So use the bridge! Our eternal destiny with God depends on this bridge, thus it is good to know that human knowledge and effort did not build the bridge. God did, because he wants us to cross over to where he is.

We know that God is not located, or limited, to some place. He is *here* as well as *there*. But this bridge I mention is a way for us finite ones to know God—to cross over into a certainty about the Invisible.

Jesus Christ is the bridge. This amazing "structure" is a person. Until we cross all the way over, we will not fully understand and appreciate what we have relied on to make that crossing. At the outset of our journey across to God, we will note that Jesus is human, and presently we see that he is also God. The bridge is a seamless structure that carries us all the way from earth to heaven, from man to God, from the visible to the invisible.

Please bear in mind that, even though this bridge is solidly anchored on our side and in our humanity, everything comes to us from the other side of the chasm. As the Son of God, our Lord always was and always is God. Then, two thousand years ago, he also became man, born of Mary in Bethlehem. The bridge is now complete—God to man—so that we in turn may get to God.

## Before I Walk, What Am I Walking On?

To venture out on Christ Jesus, our bridge to the eternal God, one needs a confidence born of truth. Our flawed and failing sight sees little of the roadway ahead.

What is the truth about Jesus that gets us underway in this greatest of all ventures—that of coming to know and be near God? Answering that question is our primary concern in the next pages. Those who stick at it, I pray, will see all of the following:

> He appeared in a body,
>    was vindicated by the Spirit,
> was seen by angels,
>    was preached among the nations,
> was believed on in the world,
>    was taken up in glory.
> (1 Tim. 3:16)

## How May I Make Personal Contact with the God of the Universe?

If you ask the question honestly about making personal contact with the God of the universe, you are already near the answer. You and I are not eternal, yet here we are, existing and questioning things. What, then, is the source of you, of me, and of all else? Let us open the Bible.

Immediately, we are informed in the opening words of the first book that creatures can know the Creator. Trouble is, however, the very first words of Scripture—"In the beginning God created"

7

(Gen. 1:1)—have become an area of doubt for many. Countless Christians live locked behind doors of doubt regarding their starting point in doctrine, namely, that God indeed exists and that this world is his creation. Without stopping to do battle here, consider the key that God offers to fit the lock on this door. It is found in John 1:3: "Through him [that is, Jesus Christ, the Son] all things were made; without him nothing was made that has been made." See also Colossians 1:16.

I must therefore settle the question of the identity of Jesus Christ if I would forever settle doubts about creation. Scripture tells me that the one who is God is also Savior, sovereign Creator, and kind Shepherd (Isa. 40:10-12). If the overwhelming distance between the God of heaven and us is not fully bridged with a clear understanding of the person and mission of Jesus, then sneaking doubts will eat away at the vitals of faith and our perception of truth, as well as our confidence in it. All down the line, doubts will hound the one whose understanding of the origin of all things is not firm and settled. But when we grant this place to Jesus Christ the Son, other insights more easily follow.

# PART 1

# GRAND TRUTHS
# NOW FUZZY

# 1

# THE MISSING ONE

I wish to show that our Lord Jesus is indeed "the missing one"—no longer convincingly present in the house of his friends. First, notice that vague teachings about Christ hang like a fog over him.

As our Mediator, Jesus is the connection between God and man, the bridge over the chasm separating the divine and the human. Or to use another figure, suggested by Scripture, he is the ladder linking heaven and earth. Precisely here we can see our double trouble. Teachers zealous to defend the deity of the Son of God have in many cases shoved up the bottom rung of the ladder until, in reality, the ladder is no longer standing on earth. Then, surprisingly enough, these same teachers, by holding to a subordination within the Trinity, have often pulled the top rung down from heaven. Let us now carefully examine this ladder set "afloat" by well-meaning Christian teachers.

## Skinned Bananas

Married less than a year, Jane and I moved to a middle-sized city in New England to found a new church. As far as I could tell, I was the only Protestant pastor living there who held to the Trinity. This very liberal stronghold boasted the daunting nickname "graveyard of evangelism." No evangelistic zeal was welcome there! We moved into a building on the south end of Main Street and began remodeling it as our chapel.

The city was stirred. "New Church!" cried the local newspaper on the front page. Hearing of our project, banks refused to lend money, even to their own customers and homeowners who were part of our flock and wished to help with the mortgage. One prominent church on North Main Street warned everyone not to get involved with us by posting this veiled jab on their corner message board: "The banana that leaves the bunch gets skinned."

My opening remark the following Sunday was, "Only the skinned banana is good to eat!" Behind the excitement was a doctrinal tension. Within the city's imposing church structures, truth was denied, actively preached against. I still have in my files samples of materials one church used to train their Sunday School teachers on how to undermine the historicity of Scripture and to explain away the supernatural. With all my strength I labored to provide an orthodox alternative. Our work prospered, and a strong church emerged.

I mention these events from more than a half-century ago to illustrate the errant doctrine that I struggled against and that is so common today. Because many in my audience had heard for years that our Lord Jesus was a noble carpenter but only a prophet-type leader, I was intent on proclaiming his absolute deity. And of course that emphasis was good and necessary. But when I read a text like Acts 10:38, which explains Jesus' wondrous works as happening "because God was with him," I so much wanted to change those words to read, "because he was God." I wanted all texts possible to shout out, "Jesus is the divine Son of God!" The Father, Son, and Holy Spirit are ever God Almighty. The trouble was, and is today, that all the hammering in one direction can cause one to lose very precious truth in the other direction.

## Dangerous Deifying of Jesus' Humanity

Both Unitarians and those who take Scripture seriously agree that Jesus lived on earth as a man. It is surprising, though, to discover that the latter sometimes do not steadfastly hold to their own teaching. Let's uncover this inconsistency.

When he lived on earth, our Lord did not demonstrate his omnipresence, a fact that causes little debate. He made the tiring trek to Samaria one step at a time. Though in his eternal deity he could be said to be everywhere present, he was not in Samaria in his body until he walked there, just as his disciples had to do. For some reason, this walking—to the point of weariness, without reliance on his omnipresence—does not seem to bother our Lord's friends today. But when it comes to his omnipotence and omniscience, that is quite another matter! Many see flashes of these attributes repeatedly.

Faithful pastors teach from Philippians 2 that when the Son of God came to earth, he laid aside the display of his deity. Then the same good pastors often reverse field and argue that Jesus' miracles (and there are lots of them!) are in fact a display of his deity. Mark 2:8 is frequently cited as such a display: "Immediately Jesus knew in his spirit that this was what they were thinking in their hearts." (When Jesus asks questions to learn information, these teachers must then feel that he has either lapsed back into human limitations or else that he is simply playacting his role as a man.) In this passage and many others, the Holy Spirit's working within our Lord's genuine human agency is too often overlooked.

The question must be faced: What exactly did Jesus lay aside, according to Philippians 2? Not his deity. (Here we all agree.) But if we say that he laid aside the display of, and reliance on, his deity, then can we turn around and take what he laid aside as proof of his deity? Obviously not! The grand truth of his deity

GRAND TRUTHS NOW FUZZY

must be established on other grounds.

After Jesus heals the man born blind, the grateful fellow testifies, "Nobody has ever heard of opening the eyes of a man born blind" (John 9:32). Next, he makes a deduction from the miracle, "If this man [that is, Jesus] were not from God, he could do nothing" (v. 33). Here is the question: Is the miracle to be explained by the fact that Jesus was *from* God, or by the fact that he *is* God? Both are true, but which is the expressed source of our Lord's earthly work?

Christ's mighty works do point us toward the conclusion that he is eternal Deity in flesh, but not in the way so often taught. Precisely here is where we have lost our Lord.

## A Doubly Serious Mistake

Basing our teaching of Jesus' deity directly on his works, miracles, and signs, rather than on his words and other Scripture, is seriously wrong on two counts: it is contrary to what Scripture actually teaches, and it compromises the realness of Christ's humanity and the integrity of the incarnation. The real Lord is thereby hidden from us—and often those most eager to defend the faith are the guilty party.

Let's now ask and answer again the important question: Are the miraculous works of Jesus the Messiah to be attributed to the Holy Spirit working through him, or are they due to our Lord's own second-person-of-the-Trinity deity? We must all agree that the Scripture teaches that Jesus is the Son of God, coequal with the Father and the Spirit. Still further, we should agree that the Son did not stop being God while on earth. Our inquiry has to do with the *manifestation* of his divine nature, now that he is joined with our humanity. What does the Bible say?

When in amazement the Jews asked concerning Jesus, "How

did this man get such learning without having studied?" Jesus gave the answer, "My teaching is not my own. It comes from him who sent me" (John 7:15-16). He later reiterated this truth when he said, "The words I say to you are not just my own. Rather, it is the Father, living in me, who is doing his work," and "These words you hear are not my own; they belong to the Father who sent me" (14:10, 24).

Keep in mind that we are asking Scripture this question: Did Jesus do his marvelous teaching and miraculous work using his resources as the divine Son of God, or did he do them as a Spirit-filled man? Peter is clear in Acts 10:38 as he taught Cornelius's household "how God anointed Jesus of Nazareth with the Holy Spirit and power, and how he went around doing good and healing all who were under the power of the devil, *because God was with him.*"

In the light of this teaching—that our Savior's wonder works were done "because God was with him"—what shall we say, then, of those who teach that Jesus hungers, sleeps, and weeps as man, but that *as God* he feeds the multitudes and rises from slumber and quiets the sea storm, and *as God* he calls Lazarus from the grave? True, only God can do these things, but what we are trying to discover is whether Jesus did these miracles as a Spirit-filled man, or whether he did them as a display of his own deity? When the staggering challenges of human needs around him would overwhelm his human resources, did he rise up as infinite God and care for the situation? Or did Jesus remain in league with us, demonstrating the power of God's Spirit working within a wholly dedicated life? Does or does not Philippians 2 teach that the Son *laid aside* the display of his majesty?

Acts 10:38 notwithstanding, some still argue that he raised the dead, thereby proving that he is God. To this I respond, please read again Acts 10:38 and consider with me the following line of reasoning for defending Christ's deity without departing from plain statements of Scripture.

Peter also raised the dead (Dorcas, see Acts 9:39-42), but when Cornelius attempted to bow before him, Peter stopped him, saying, "I am only a man myself" (Acts 10:26). Peter's works prove that he is a Spirit-filled man. You can trust the words of a Spirit-filled man, and he says, "I am only a man." By the same token, you can trust the words of Jesus Christ, whose works certify that he is God's Spirit-filled human representative, and he teaches us that he is the divine Son of God. That is how we know with certainty that the Lord Jesus is God. Our human nature likes to stake all on miracles and signs, but Jesus said, "Blessed are those who have not seen and yet have believed" (John 20:29).

God simply has not given such a crucial place to signs and wonders that the proof of our Lord's eternal deity should rest on these. No, it rests ultimately on his word, as he insists in John 8:24, "If you do not believe that I am the one I claim to be, you will indeed die in your sins." The Gospel of John stands out in Scripture for its affirmation of Christ's eternal deity as the Son of God. Yet this same book repeatedly quotes our Lord as he claims true humanity, and his message is used to set forth his identity as Messiah. Here is a sample:

> "Who are you?" they asked.
>
> "Just what I have been claiming all along," Jesus replied. "I have much to say in judgment of you. But he who sent me is reliable, and what I have heard from him I tell the world."
>
> They did not understand that he was telling them about his Father. So Jesus said, "When you have lifted up the Son of Man, then you will know that I am the one I claim to be [the Messiah, God's Son] and that I do nothing

on my own but speak just what the Father has taught me.
The one who sent me is with me; he has not left me alone,
for I always do what pleases him." Even as he spoke, many
put their faith in him.

To the Jews who had believed him, Jesus said, "If you
hold to my teaching, you are really my disciples. Then you
will know the truth, and the truth will set you free." (John
8:25-32)

Shortly after the above pronouncement, Jesus describes
himself to his foes as "a man who has told you the truth that
I heard from God" (John 8:40). To miss his message is to
misunderstand who he is.

Christ did not live a life removed from the dusty way of
ordinary human existence. He did not periodically shift into the
display-of-deity mode. "Because he himself suffered when he was
tempted, he is able to help those who are being tempted" (Heb.
2:18). Then rejoice, believers, in our Lord's genuine human
nature and—apart from our sin—in his complete identity with
us: "For we do not have a high priest who is unable to sympathize
with our weaknesses, but we have one who has been tempted in
every way, just as we are—yet was without sin" (Heb. 4:15).

Yes, Jesus is most certainly the eternal, infinite Son of God,
but he became man also and lived within the bounds of human
resources (having to use physical energy, brain, and walking from
one place to another) instead of relying on, and demonstrating,
his own divine resources (omnipotence, omniscience, and
omnipresence). Hebrews 5:7-9 makes it dramatically clear:
"During the days of Jesus' life on earth, he offered up prayers
and petitions with loud cries and tears. . . . He learned obedience
from what he suffered and, once made perfect, he became the
source of eternal salvation for all who obey him."

How grateful we are that our Savior did not disconnect from us by reaching back into his own eternal resources when he faced challenges on earth. At Lazarus's grave, before he called the dead man to rise, he first prayed to his Father in heaven. Consequently, when we see the mighty power of the Holy Spirit, we are thereby encouraged in our faith and stirred to follow him in a close contact of prayer. Study carefully John 14:12-14:

> I tell you the truth, anyone who has faith in me will do what I have been doing. He will do even greater things than these, because I am going to the Father. And I will do whatever you ask in my name, so that the Son may bring glory to the Father. You may ask me for anything in my name, and I will do it.

Before moving on, let's recapitulate. Consider these three truths about Jesus that should help us maintain the integrity of his incarnation. First, his real birth provides a genuine humanity. Second, his real life proves a genuine humanity. Third, his real suffering and death require a genuine humanity. In relation to this third point, we all know that God can neither lie nor die. But Christ *died*. This fact places a special guard about his human nature. While we must maintain the unity and integrity of his personhood, Calvary's death requires us to affirm the genuineness of his human nature. (See appendix 1 for discussion of whether we can say that *God* died on the cross.)

## Does the Ladder Reach All the Way Up?

Having established the integrity of Christ's humanity, let's now make sure that faulty notions about his subordination within the Trinity do not hinder our own relationship with him as our Mediator.

It is commonly said that Jesus is 100 percent God and

100 percent man. I think I know what speakers mean by this statement, but these words in themselves encourage hearers to accept a vague confusion (100 percent + 100 percent = *200* percent). Is it not better to say that the Lord is truly God but that he also has become man? From all eternity the Son is ever God; then a couple thousand years ago, he also took on humanity.

Numbers of times I have heard persons who would claim to be very sound in their biblical faith teach error regarding the subordination of Jesus Christ. They often do so on the basis of Scriptures like John 14:28, where Jesus said, "If you loved me, you would be glad that I am going to the Father, for the Father is greater than I." A group of thirty-five respected pastors discussed this very text in my hearing some years ago. So far as I could tell, not one, including the leader, sided with me. All felt that the Son was subordinate to the Father both on earth *and in eternity.* During a break, I dashed to the nearby office of the resident professor of theology. Hearing of the position taken by the discussion leader, he said quietly, "My colleague is wrong."

True enough, Jesus obeyed his parents, paid taxes, prayed to God, and yielded to his will, even to death on the cross, but this submission must not be understood so as to contradict his words in John 10:30, "I and the Father are one," or the words of Paul about Christ, "Who, being in very nature God, did not consider *equality with God* something to be grasped, but made himself nothing, taking the very nature of a servant, being made in human likeness" (Phil. 2:6-7).

Simply put, Does the Scripture emphasize the Son's subordination within the Godhead, the Trinity, or does the teaching have primary reference to his role as the incarnate Redeemer? The latter is true. Sonship does not imply eternal, essential subordination to the Father; rather, the term "Son" sets forth equality and union in one essence. Remember the apostle's comments in John 5:18, "For this reason the Jews tried all the harder to kill him; not only was he breaking the Sabbath, but he was even calling God his own Father, making himself equal with God."

However we understand the functional relation of the Father and the Son as it was in eternity, we must not press this relation back into the essence, or eternal substance, of God. Consider how carefully the Father balances truths about his Son in Hebrews 1, when he says, beginning at verse 5, "You are my Son; today I have become your Father," Here he is speaking of the human birth of the Messiah, with all the admiration and approval of the Father in heaven. The next verse adds the command "Let all God's angels worship him." Verse 8 follows with, "But about the Son he [God, the Father] says, 'Your throne, O God, will last for ever and ever.'" Not only are angels ordered to worship the Son, but the Father addresses the Son as God.

There is no such thing as being, in the same sense, both "equal with" and "less than." Yet there are some who want the mediatorial ladder to reach to the Tri-Unity, while they at the same time give strong emphasis to the Son's subordination to the Father prior to creation back in all eternity. Within the essence of the Godhead, there is no variation or gradation or alteration. God in substance is pure One, a perfect Unity, and absolutely immutable.

The plurality of the persons of the Trinity does not imply gradation or divisions within the Godhead: "The Father of the heavenly lights . . . does not change like shifting shadows" (James 1:17). Reference to the three persons as first, second, and third enables our finite minds to think in an orderly fashion and avoid confusion, but the terms do not indicate High, Middle, Low.

It would be helpful if teachers would cease speaking of any one of the three as "part" of the Trinity. The Godhead has no parts! Rather, all three (persons) participate fully in the one (essence). (Don't forget the fundamental text Deut. 6:4: "Hear, O Israel: The LORD our God, the LORD is *one.*") The Father, Son, and Holy Spirit are members, not parts, of the Godhead. The one being is indivisible and immutable. Furthermore, the incarnation brought no alteration in the essence of God.

All must admit that fully explaining and grasping the Trinity is beyond human capacities. But that limitation is no excuse for abandoning the revealed insights given us by God and turning to such typical statements as, "We can't understand the Trinity—how God is three and yet one—but we accept it by faith." This treatment forces the poor listeners to make a terrible choice between believing a sheer contradiction or having a defective faith regarding the Trinity.

It is far better to say that God is three in one way, and one in another way. He is one as to his essence, and three as to persons. Three persons participating equally, fully in the one essence. God is one being existing in the three distinct persons. You and I are one-person beings, but God is a three-person being. It ought not surprise us to learn that God is different from us. Furthermore, his wondrous being can be known only through his Word, as the Spirit of truth enlightens us. Remember, we are talking of *revealed* truth. God's revelation is not confusion. Surely, we are not burdened with having to overcome an apparent contradiction by some kind of tenacious faith.

God is knowable because he is a self-revealing Deity. The grand truth of God's existence is embraced and understood by faith arising from Scripture and confirmed in experience. The data that feeds faith, then, is God's Word and all his works in providence and creation. At the heart of it all stands our Lord Jesus Christ, the Son of God, who is the living Word of God.

## Will We Ever See God?

That the question about ever seeing God is still being asked 2,000 years after Jesus gave his answer to it proves how dimly we see and know him. "Don't you know me, Philip, even after I have been among you such a long time? Anyone who has seen me has seen the Father. How can you say, 'Show us the Father'? Don't you believe that I am in the Father, and that the Father is in me? The words I say to you are not just my own. Rather, it is the Father, living in me, who is doing his work" (John 14:9-10).

This Jesus, who is the supreme Message of God to mankind, is said to be also "the radiance of God's glory and the exact representation of his being" (Heb. 1:3). He was called Immanuel, which means, "God with us" (Matt. 1:23). Jesus came forth from Mary's womb in our nature and likeness—"he appeared in a body" (1 Tim. 3:16)—and yet with perfect fidelity he manifested God to us: "He is the image of the invisible God" (Col. 1:15).

Image worship is sternly forbidden in the Bible, but when it comes to our Lord Jesus as the image of God, we *must* worship. He is God, come to us in human nature; he has taken the decisive position as Mediator between God and man. This means that he both represents God to us and represents us to God. At this point we are dealing with the former. We will deal with the latter when we take up the study of our Lord's ascension and how we approach God as we pray in Jesus' name.

We see that both the person and the work of Christ are involved in the matter of his being the image of God to us. In order to bring us into contact with the true God, this one divine being not only must be truly God but also must show his divine nature living and working in real human nature. The disciple John wrote about this truly human Jesus:

> That which was from the beginning, which we have heard, which we have seen with our eyes, which we have looked at and our hands have touched—this we proclaim concerning the Word of life. The life appeared; we have seen it and testify to it, and we proclaim to you the eternal life, which was with the Father and has appeared to us. We proclaim to you what we have seen and heard, so that you also may have fellowship with us. And our fellowship is with the Father and with his Son, Jesus Christ. We write this to make our joy complete. (1 John 1:1-4)

Though Almighty God is infinite, invisible, and not limited to any physical boundaries that would let us "locate" him with our senses, he has reached out to us visibly by the incarnation of Jesus Christ. Through Jesus' humanity, we can know God, "for God was pleased to have all his fullness dwell in him" (Col. 1:19); again, "In Christ all the fullness of the Deity lives in bodily form" (Col. 2:9). This means that the ladder stands firmly where we stand—in earth's soil—and reaches all the way to the triune Godhead. Get hold of even the bottom rung of the ladder, and you will be transformed. Jesus promises, "When a man believes in me, he does not believe in me only, but in the one who sent me. When he looks at me, he sees the one who sent me. I have come into the world as a light, so that no one who believes in me should stay in darkness" (John 12:44-46).

In the opening words of his gospel account, John introduces the Son of God as the Word. He is ever the Revelation, Expression, or Great Message of God. But his assignment to image God to us involves more than words: "When Christ came into the world, he said: 'Sacrifice and offering you did not desire, but a body you prepared for me'" (Heb. 10:5). Or as John puts it, "The Word became flesh and made his dwelling among us. We have seen his glory, the glory of the One and Only, who came from the Father, full of grace and truth" (John 1:14).

Having a body and human nature enables Jesus to image, or mirror, God directly to us in many dimensions in addition to the visual. The problem is that "he was in the world, and though the world was made through him, the world did not recognize him" (John 1:10). Our concern here, however, is not only what the world thinks, but especially how believers are misunderstanding, or misrepresenting and mistreating, their Lord.

## Damage Assessment

Harm done to the church by the blurred teachings about our Lord's person is perhaps beyond estimating, but let us attempt some assessment.

Jesus once said, "Now this is eternal life: that they may know you, the only true God, and Jesus Christ, whom you have sent" (John 17:3). See how important this knowing is! "Whenever anyone turns to the Lord, the veil is taken away. . . . And we, who with unveiled faces all reflect the Lord's glory, are being transformed into his likeness with ever-increasing glory, which comes from the Lord, who is the Spirit" (2 Cor. 3:16, 18). The apostle adds in 4:6, "For God, who said, 'Let light shine out of darkness,' made his light shine in our hearts to give us the light of the knowledge of the glory of God in the face of Christ." In the light of these promises, why the dullness and ineffectiveness of contemporary believers? Perhaps many do not *see* much of Jesus. This means they *know* incorrectly. And therefore they *show* little.

Recall our illustration of Jesus as the ladder. If his mediation does not reach all the way into our very humanity on the one end, and if it does not extend into absolute equality with the Father at the other end, we have lost the real Lord Jesus Christ, and we are out of touch with God.

By saying that our Lord's powerful works came from his own deity, not from the Spirit working within him, teachers obscure our understanding of the Spirit's work in Jesus. We are then set adrift in this world without a Savior whose example is in our league. How crucial is the damage done by those who, in their press to assert our Lord's deity, give up his true manhood! Both his deity and his manhood must be held securely.

Again, those who teach must be careful not to sully the doctrine of the Son's eternal deity when they speak of a subordination that existed prior to creation—before anything existed "outside" of God. When closely questioned, too many among the ranks of believers hold that the Son is less than the Father. Those who would be custodians of Trinitarian doctrine must make very sure that they do not appear to be placing the Son below the Father. Unguarded teaching in this area of doctrine is responsible for the sad, unthinking drift of many into serious error regarding God's Son. The burden of responsibility is surely on all of us, while teaching the condescension of the Son, to make clear that the subordination does not extend to the substance of the eternal Godhead.

In the following pages, we will examine several other serious errors. They concern our Lord's work of atonement, intercession, rule, and headship of the church, as well as our service for him in evangelism and in the various dimensions of edifying and sustaining others. If we are sent as he was sent (see John 20:21), any cloudiness in our view of Jesus' person and work will greatly hinder our effort to represent and serve him.

Vaguely defined truth cannot be defended. Instead, it is lost.

Wherever truth is lost, strongly voiced proclamations using well-illustrated points do not make things right.

A particular focus of difficulty will be seen in the area of prayer. Ready, confident access to the Father depends very much on what we learn from Jesus' real, Spirit-filled, human life and our present alignment with him, and from Jesus' present place with the Father. Some of the additional problems to be unearthed will be simply consequences of errors already mentioned. Others will be "new," but all ultimately derive from a faulty handling of the truth about the Lord Jesus Christ.

## Review and Appeal

The Son of God truly humbled himself and became one of us, apart from our sinful bent. Though he never ceased to be God, he lived on earth within the bounds of human resources, with the support of the Holy Spirit.

Although he now has both divine and human natures, our Lord is one person. On earth he rightfully accepted Thomas's worship (addressing Jesus as "my Lord and my God," John 20:28), and he taught that he is the Son of God. This truth, though, came by revelation, not by demonstration of miracles (see Matt. 16:16-17).

Jesus, then, is the supreme Revealer of God. If this truth should be confused and lost to our understanding, we likely also will lose a firm grasp on his life and work as Redeemer and Ruler.

As pictured earlier, many of the faithful are left holding empty bottles. Instead of being filled with potent truth, they contain mostly just air. Labels are to some extent correct and orthodox, but what power resides in the paper? It is not good to live "having a form of godliness but denying its power" (2 Tim. 3:5).

We have only begun our story, but already I trust it will be apparent that getting these matters right and bringing Christ back to his place should take priority over so many other things. For example, how can we genuinely look for the Lord's second coming when to such a degree we have obscured his first coming?

# 2

# IS SIN WHAT
# YOU THINK IT IS?

"Come on, please! Let's get on with it. I would expect the least member in my church to know the definition of sin!"

This gruff interruption of my address gained everyone's attention. I was the host pastor of the local ministers' meeting and had been invited to speak on a topic of my choosing. No sooner had I announced that my chosen subject was "Clarifying Our Definition of Sin" than the young pastor directly in front of me burst out with his complaint.

Being young myself, I rose to the occasion with a challenge: "Just as the word 'cancer' may have different meanings," I said, "so 'sin' is used in the Bible in different ways. In fact, there are three very distinct aspects to the large subject of sin. Now, I make the challenge that not one of you can give an adequate, useful definition of sin, distinguishing these three aspects of the subject." Immediately, I handed out notepaper to each and requested a response in writing.

Granted, my approach was impolite, but I made my point with these friends. Their papers revealed only typical phrases— well-worn and unhelpful. In fact, over the decades in which I have put this question to Christian leaders and followers, I do not recall meeting a single one who seemed ready with a complete answer. Without exception, however, all felt that the subject of sin was fairly simple, a basic doctrine that they had well in hand.

Here, then, is my challenging objective: to show that the doctrine of sin is of profound scope and importance and yet is little understood. This lack of understanding arises from the fact that the great root system of humanity's sinful plight lies hidden, unexposed. To spur us on in our pursuit, dear reader, will you not agree with me in advance that in order to preach the cross of Christ with its full power, we must be clear about what mankind's problem is that Jesus' sacrifice is intended to remedy?

## Defining Sin

As we ponder this topic, an obvious question arises: How does sin get through all generations to (and into) me and to (and into) you? Like a relentless tidal wave, sweeping over every person of the human family, the condition of sin engulfs every participant in human history. Our ability to know God is ruined. He becomes hopelessly mysterious and distant. Though God is infinite and the best-evidenced fact of the universe (see Rom. 1:18-20), our broken spiritual sight perceives him only with an indistinct haziness.

Sin is our total condition of trouble, leaving us disjointed from God, often alienated from others, and unable to live as we ought. Every personal faculty has been rendered imperfect by this malignant ailment called sin, and every dimension of society has been disturbed. To fix this sorry mess—or rather to fix us— Christ came. And the redemption he brings must go to the root of things.

Today's weak view of the cross, held by those who count themselves as Christ's friends and true preachers of the cross, will remain undetected and never made right as long as we have a faulty, imprecise definition of sin. A bit of confident talk is a poor substitute for a proper definition of sin in its three major aspects. Once the depth of sin's meaning is clarified, the manner of its transmission to each offspring will become clear. Clarity on this point will make possible a new and powerful understanding of the cross, something we need if we are to have a full and settled peace with God. Seeing sin as it really is, in God's eyes, makes redemption stand out all the more clearly.

The truth is, all the evil we observe comes from an inner brokenness and sinful bent that, in turn, arises from a hidden, unobservable condition. To get at that deepest level, we must see more clearly our relation to Adam and what he did.

## More than a Tragic Tumble

We feel involved somehow in the sad loss of Eden's paradise. When Adam and Eve were shut out, their loss became our loss. Children inherit what their parents leave behind. Like a family holding hands as they climb a steep, icy hill, a careless step by the father not only causes his own fall but also drags down all his clan with him.

Adam's fall was not carelessness but a matter of choice. God warned, "You must not eat from the tree of the knowledge of good and evil, for when you eat of it you will surely die" (Gen. 2:17). Not "*if* you eat" but "*when* [lit. *in the day*] you eat." The promised punishment of death was to be exacted at the time of the transgression. Stopping breathing is by no means the full issue. Adam lived on for many years, but he died *when* he ate—in his character—as a poisoning depravity spread throughout his person. The biblical account gives ample evidence of this death, even as he lived on. For Adam and Eve, the presence of God was no longer their delight but their dread. Suspicion and accusations developed between the two of them.

Then it was to their horror, I am sure, that the blight of sin burst forth in the life of Cain, their firstborn son. He murdered his brother Abel in cold blood. How could this happen? Their precious Cain a murderer! What in his environment could explain such a development? Or what in his genetics? Nothing. This inner blight is not "caught" from people or things around us, nor is it piped in through blood relations. Sin is not some kind of physical infection. It may impact the physical and other realms, but that is not its root essence.

Let's now give more definition to the large subject of sin. There are three major divisions to this subject. The first two are commonly spoken of, but not the third. Yet this third aspect is the hugely important hidden root, supporting and giving rise to everything about our problem with evil. After directly reviewing the first two aspects of the doctrine of sin, I will make a more gradual approach to this third aspect, seeking to prove that herein is the root of the whole matter. Only then can the other truths yet to be shared be solidly based.

## Sin as Wrongdoing

The most obvious division of the large subject of sin involves actions that God condemns as wrong. The simple statement "All wrongdoing is sin" (1 John 5:17) is clear. This aspect of the subject must be filled out to include both what is committed and what is omitted—in word, thought, and deed. Two other texts, from many, are similar: "Anyone, then, who knows the good he ought to do and doesn't do it, sins" (James 4:17), and "Everyone who sins breaks the law; in fact, sin is lawlessness" (1 John 3:4).

Romans 3:23 is very familiar to most Bible readers, but the

truth is still shocking when we are told that, without exception, "*all* have sinned and fall short of the glory of God." The universality of wrongdoing forces us to ask why we all sin. God's Word leads us to understand that our wrongdoing comes from some defilement deep within that corrupts the good and moves us into the wrong.

## Sin as Inner Defilement

King David was keenly aware of the aspect of sin as inner defilement, which we can see in his touching psalm of confession: "Surely I was sinful at birth, sinful from the time my mother conceived me" (Ps. 51:5).

The New Testament throws much light on this use of "sin" as our inner bias toward evil. Romans 7:16-20 explains that wrongdoing and selfishness are natural: "And if I do what I do not want to do, I agree that the law is good. As it is, it is no longer I myself who do it, but it is sin living in me. I know that nothing good lives in me, that is, in my sinful nature. For I have the desire to do what is good, but I cannot carry it out. For what I do is not the good I want to do; no, the evil I do not want to do—this I keep on doing. Now if I do what I do not want to do, it is no longer I who do it, but it is sin living in me that does it."

Twice we are told here that it is not "I" doing the sinful acts, "but it is sin living in me." This means that the apostle does not agree with those who speak of the "sinful I" as if the core of my being is sin. I am under condemnation and also depraved, but my essence is not sin, though I might be declared to be sinful. Sin attaches to me in experience, but languishing in this plight is a core of being that God reaches to redeem. God does not eradicate, educate, or salvage my sinful nature, but he does move to redeem *me*.

Examining Paul's words, we see that our volition is enslaved by sin and pressed into the service of evil desires. Thus it is the inner defilement that leads to wrongdoing.

## The Key Question

Where does this crippling inner corruption come from? Now we are asking the key question in our pursuit!

To begin our inquiry, think back for a moment. Have you not at some time heard an evangelist appeal to the love of God by telling the listeners, "If you had been the only one on earth, Christ would still have come to die for you—so great is his love." We can accept this point. But now let's modify this hypothetical statement for our use: If the only person on earth were an infant, would Christ come and die for that infant? Yes, I would say. But what defect would this baby have that would require the death of the Savior on the cross?

I think we can agree that infants have some kind of problem, for every child born in the world grows up to violate the light and standards of Scripture; every infant must be restrained from lying, angry outbursts and the like. They can do evil without help, but to do right they need help. We must ask again, How did this evil bent, or drive, get there?

## Unhelpful Answers

"From the environment," some will answer, thinking of imperfect parents, evil companions, and similar influences. But that is only to put off the question, which then becomes, Since people to a large extent make up and control the environment, how did sin get into all their lives, and thence to us?

To answer this question, those who ought to know Bible truth but who only vaguely define sin usually content themselves with vague and fuzzy, if not skewed, notions. I have often heard expressions such as "We are born in sin" or "We have inherited sin." I know from years of questioning people in discipling sessions that they are thinking of this inherited evil almost as though it were some corkscrew-like flaw in their genetic system! But how could our physical DNA be the source of our moral evil? We need to look in other directions to find out how this terrible inheritance is forced upon us unwilling heirs.

Let's return now to our original human father. Recall that Adam was not born, he was made—directly by God. The first baby birthed into this world, Cain, grew up to be a murderer, as he killed the next-born, his brother Abel. Where did Cain's murderous heart come from? How was it transmitted into him?

## Sin as Legal Guilt

We come now, finally, to the root aspect of our subject: sin as legal guilt. It has everything to do with Adam, our ultimate human legal head.

Already we have observed that when Adam disobeyed, he died. First he died inwardly, in his personal character, and ultimately the grave claimed his body. Death, then—in both aspects—is the penalty, the punishment for sin, just as Romans 6:23 instructs us: "For the wages of sin is death." The implications are clear regarding the rest of mankind, all of whom are suffering the very same punishment within. This infliction is because we are counted by the Judge of all as being truly guilty. *But why is this so?*

The ultimate damning problem is not our physical connection with Adam but our legal connection with him. The key truth is lodged in the phrase "in Adam all die" (1 Cor. 15:22). Death (sin's penalty) is inflicted on the guilty, who are said to be "in Adam." This use of the preposition "in" here is intended to convey to us that we are counted judicially in Adam, in his lineage. Apart from our rights or our wills, our birth decides who our legal father is and what our name and inheritance are to be. We are born *of* our father and are thus *in* him. His is ours. We cannot step into a neighbor's family line and inheritance in order to change our own. Our problem is that Adam and all his line are in a state of sin. We cannot get back into the paradise of Eden. When Adam lost it, we all lost it. All of Adam's line are born where he was after his sin—under the canopy of guilt.

It must follow that all who are guilty will experience the penalty—death. As we have noted, this death is twofold—first in our character, and finally death in our body. That is why each infant grows up to display the deceitful heart of sin, a brokenness in character. Guilt is already there, and so the punishment of death must follow. It is extremely important that we keep in mind that this powerful inner corruption of character is to be viewed as the first stroke of the sentence of death. Romans 5:12 shows how Adam's fall into sin was our fall too: "Therefore, just as sin entered the world through one man, and death through sin, . . . in this way death came to all men, because all sinned."

**One, Two, Three**

Looking again at the three uses of the important term "sin," we are now prepared to place them in order. Every human being is born "in Adam" and thus shares his (1) *sin as legal guilt*. The penalty is inherent, which means that all, from birth, bear the blight of (2) *sin as inner defilement*. Such brokenness in character will issue in (3) *sin as wrongdoing*.

These three strands of such a major subject as sin must be separated and given clear definition, or else woeful weaknesses will debilitate the grand doctrines that stand under the headings of our Lord's person and work. I will say it even more pointedly: Unless one's view of mankind's legal jeopardy is seen as the great taproot of mankind's problem, the other issues of sin will never yield fully to all the preaching and teaching we might muster. What is worse, our Lord himself will not be correctly viewed, the heart of his work will be bypassed, and believers will be left to wobble their way through life, victimized by sin made more powerful by weak and vague definition. Unless there is a recovery of this lost truth, our problems will only be compounded from beginning to end, as I will seek to show. Conversely, if we humbly own up to our slackness with the truth and set our hearts to change, we can indeed *bring Christ back.*

Two imposing problems, which will surely loom in the minds of many readers at this juncture, are surveyed in the appendixes. One concerns the salvation of infants who die. If babies are under guilt and thus liable to death, then how are they saved? (See appendix 2.) The other issue, addressed in appendix 3, concerns the problem of evil in God's world, specifically, the origin, extent, and end of evil.

# 3

# GOD'S SON AND OUR SIN

Sweeping like a flood from one generation to the next, the irresistible onslaught of sin stopped suddenly at Mary's womb when Jesus was conceived. Remarkably enough, however, the dark tide engulfed Mary's other children, for Scripture tells us that they grew up disbelieving and hostile to Jesus. Obviously, then, our Lord's sinless character cannot be explained on the basis of Mary's sanctity.

Matthew's account of Jesus' conception (1:18-25) shows how God protected his Son from sin. Joseph was excluded from the conception, and Jesus was sired instead by a miraculous intervention of God: "Before they [Mary and Joseph] came together [as husband and wife], she was found to be with child through the Holy Spirit" (v. 18).

The conception thus excluded Joseph but included Mary. As soon as Joseph took his natural role in fathering the other children, sin prevailed over them. Some have therefore erroneously concluded that sin is somehow passed genetically from father to child. But as we saw in chapter 2, sin in its essence is not genetic, physical material.

By standing Joseph aside, God could then declare to Mary through the angel, "The Holy Spirit will come upon you, and the power of the Most High will overshadow you. So the holy one to be born will be called the Son of God" (Luke 1:35). Jesus' human lineage as it came through Mary, then, did not involve him in the guilt of our forefather Adam. Jesus was born as "the *holy* one."

In stark contrast, every single person in Adam's line is guilty and condemned. This condemnation brings the penalty of death in a baby's personal character and also brings liability to the shadows of the grave. That guilt is a *legal* inheritance and is decreed through every father to each child.

To review: a father sires the children, while the mother bears the children. Both mother and father share in genetic input to the child. Both contribute to the physical makeup of each offspring. But it is the father alone who gives his name and legal status to the child. The inheritance—the spiritual status—comes from him.

Being conceived by the Holy Spirit and without an earthly father, Jesus was therefore without sin's guilt and its penalty. No death was due Jesus Christ, either in his person or physically. He was born perfectly pure within, and the death he ultimately died was not required of him for his own guilt but for a guilt assigned to him on our behalf.

### New Light from Jesus
Looking through the lens of Jesus' life exposes the nature of sin more clearly. The guilt of sin is such that (1) it could be kept from Jesus by the exclusion of an earthly father and family head and (2) it can be lifted from us and assigned to our Savior in his atonement for us. The main mystery about sin is clarified by looking more closely at our Lord Jesus Christ, at his person and work.

The primary, root concern about sin is its legal, forensic issue. Since our human lineage traces back to Adam, the family head who has brought judgment on himself and his line, we inherit the legal guilt of Adam's sin. Thankfully, Jesus was not rooted in Adam but in heaven. "I have come down from heaven" (John 6:38), he said repeatedly. Therefore, no penalty for guilt was due him, and being free from the punishment of inner defilement, he never showed an inclination to wrongdoing. Rather, he showed the likeness of his Father in heaven.

## Our Big Question: Can We Somehow Escape from Our Own Family Tree?

Here is the situation: It is impossible for us to quit all our sinful attitudes and actions unless we have God's help with the sinful nature within us, and he won't bring about this sanctifying work until our guilt is made right. This right standing with God that we so desperately need requires a true release from Adam's guilt. We most certainly are guilty, because the judgment of the death sentence is passed on all Adam's line in one divine declaration. Already we are experiencing the initial phase of that death sentence in the form of a pervading blight in our character. Physical death is next. We are utterly without hope unless a way can be found to change our very family line.

Now, changing our lineage is a huge, far-reaching matter, but that is what must occur if we are to be saved. It's like reaching all the way back into our past, to the beginning of all history, pulling up our roots, and planting ourselves in a new line. Or we could say it this way: Christ saves us by settling our sin accounts with God in such a way that God is pleased to bring us into another birth—born of God, into Jesus Christ's line!

Here I want to make it very plain that the new birth involves far more than fixing our flawed history of wrongdoing. And it is much more than a cleansing of our inner defilement or pollution, which results from the death sentence we all receive as children of Adam. Christian salvation, at its root, is a change in the legal registry of each one who believes in Christ.

## Christian Impostors?

Imagine for a moment that a hunted lawbreaker decides to make a new start. He wants more than a change in his lifestyle. He attempts to change family lines—to get into an upright, noble lineage. He has two significant problems, however. First, the law is after him; he is guilty. Second, he can't move in and "borrow" a nice family name. No one will have him.

So many today borrow the name that is above all names, that of Jesus Christ. But they won't get away with it. No matter what changes they attempt or how active they are within the Christian household—perhaps living there as squatters for years—the same two significant problems cry out against them, just as with the lawbreaker mentioned above.

The very thought of writing oneself into God's family line is preposterous, for two reasons. First, *all are guilty before God.* We are guilty, not only for what we may have done, but for who we are, back to our roots. We are part of a parentage of sin. Our whole tribe is under the curse of the almighty Judge. The law is after us until a just settlement is made. In addition, *We cannot push ourselves, or earn our way, into God's family.* Trying to live like a child of God when not really in his line with his life flowing in us is terribly stressful, although the large number who are making that attempt perhaps provide a measure of false comfort to each other.

As we prepare now to look carefully at the cross of Christ, we will discover directly how God makes our spiritual roots right and eternal. But before new life and vitality are fully ours, we must free ourselves from a mass of tangled, weedlike teachings that have, by years of unchecked growth, gained acceptance as biblical truth. Let us proceed carefully. First, review the definition of sin in its three aspects:

1. the root issue of our universal guilt in Adam
2. the infliction of that guilt's punishment, which brings spiritual death within us (corrupting us and inclining us to sin) and ultimately physical death
3. the expression of our sinful nature in wrong attitudes and actions.

Next, we must consider how the death of Christ remedies our sinful lot. The remedy (redemption) is applied first at the root and proceeds from there to the other two aspects of sin.

## Recovering the Lost Work of Christ

Join me in imagining a court scene where you and I are facing the judge. You and I both are guilty of a serious crime, and we admit it to the court. Now here is a riddle with a stunning biblical application: How is it possible for the magistrate to be a just judge and let us go free if we are admittedly guilty? We do not want our earthly judges to bend justice. All the more, then, shall not God do right? How is it possible for God to declare the guilty innocent?

Many answer, "Because God is love." That explanation is commonly given, but it is very wrong as an answer to our question. Scripture does not tell us that God loves us so much that he simply forgives our sin. No. We are taught, rather, that he loves us so much that he provides a just settlement for our guilt: "But God demonstrates his own love for us in this: While we were still sinners, Christ died for us" (Rom. 5:8).

The truth is, God forgives those guilty ones who believe

41

in Jesus Christ *because he is just.* Once the Redeemer has made payment on our behalf, it would be unjust for the Judge to require further payment; therefore, "he is faithful and just and will forgive us our sins" (1 John 1:9). Forgiveness is granted on the basis of a satisfied justice, at the instigation of love.

## Focusing on the Main Thing

The two most common and general problems troubling our spiritual life are a guilty conscience, with a resulting dread of having to answer to the holy God, and our weak resistance to temptations fertilized by inner evil desires, making for continual lapses into sin. How do we escape from this brokenness and misery?

No matter what degree of pain we might experience in these two regards, the main thing about sin is not its bother to you and me but its offense to God, the Righteous One. He declares the sinful one guilty and condemned. This state of damnation is exposed in the Bible as being the root condition of sin—sin as legal guilt. Jesus came into our world and died as a sacrifice for our sins in order to resolve this main issue first.

Until sin is properly defined, the cross of Christ will forever be slighted, by friend and foe alike. When the cross is clearly viewed and embraced as the just settlement for guilt, sin's inner malignancy can then be dealt with, and the resulting evils in behavior can be stayed—but not until then!

Or we could state the issue another way. Our sins are more than crimes against society, the government, courts, or any earthly official. They are against God. We break his laws and offend his infinite righteousness. Beyond what we do or what we are within our hearts, we are spiritual aliens and enemies to God. Thus we are designated as guilty and are already sentenced to death.

As we have seen, this death is more than stopping breathing; it involves a corruption in every dimension of our character, so deep that we are unable to extricate ourselves or to escape our sinful state. Ultimately, we must sink into the grave and face God in a personal accounting.

One thing should be obvious by now—the legal charges must be met, or there can never be a removal of the penalty we are already enduring and the penalty that is yet ahead in eternity. But how can all sin's charges be lifted from us?

Let us try picturing ourselves as a condemned prisoner. As we sit in the darkened cell awaiting our doom, we go over and over our few options:

1. We might try to be a model prisoner, obeying the rules. (But any future good deeds won't undo our existing debt of guilt.)
2. We might hold to a hope that the judge won't be just. (But our Judge is always perfectly just.)
3. We might give up and simply face the judgment and punishment that is due us. (But we know we don't want this option!)
4. Or we might pray for a rescue of some sort. It would indeed be wonderful if a savior would intervene who could satisfy justice and bring release to us.

Our Savior has in fact accomplished this fourth option for us—on the cross.

In our day, however, preaching about the blood offering of Jesus satisfying God's justice is being set aside for more contemporary themes, or else the message is buried by loads of familiar, indefinite, inadequate phrases. As a result, the death of our Lord for sin is no longer the powerful center of the Christian faith. It is said to be, but it is not shown to be.

Let's begin our recovery effort with a simple diagram that has proven helpful to many (see fig. 1). It highlights the twofold direction of Jesus' work on the cross.

**The Two Works of Christ**

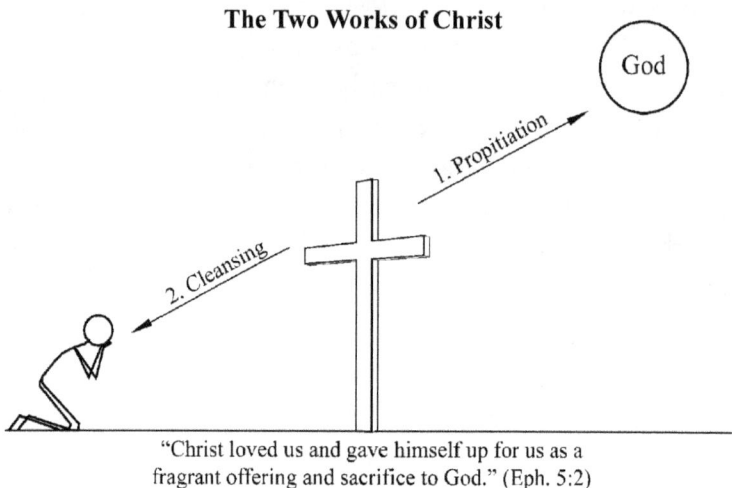

"Christ loved us and gave himself up for us as a fragrant offering and sacrifice to God." (Eph. 5:2)

Figure 1

Focus on the two prepositional phrases "for us" and "to God" in Ephesians 5:2: "Christ loved us and gave himself up *for us* as a fragrant offering and sacrifice *to God*." Notice that the way in which he gave himself "for us" was as an offering "to God." That which he rendered "to God" is given "for us." The supreme thing Jesus did "for us" was to make this payment "to God" on our behalf.

Jesus did not die for us simply as a favor we needed. The power of what he did lies in its Godward direction. Study prayerfully the two numbered arrows in the diagram. When the Godward impact of the cross is not fully emphasized, people will come to feel that the manward impact of the cross is the basis of their right standing with God. In other words, step 1 (propitiation) can seem dependent on step 2 (cleansing). This is serious error! It is not enough simply to agree with this evaluation. The right order must be understood and emphasized.

## A Shadowy Substitution?

As painful as it is to hear teachers reject Christ's death as a vicarious substitution for us sinners, it is perhaps more frustrating to hear those who insist on right terminology slide into popular, worn grooves of talk that misses the main thing.

When I say "Christ died for me," I am saying more than that he did it as a favor for me. Also I am saying more than that he took the punishment for my sin. And it is still insufficient to proclaim that he died "in my place" if I do not make it clear what these crucial words "in my place" mean. Those coming to Jesus for salvation need to know that the Savior is their stand-in, that he died in their stead, in their very name, as their officially designated Substitute. Therefore, we believers can say with understanding, Christ was assigned my guilt and paid my penalty. My record of condemnation is imputed (that is, attributed or accredited) to Jesus: "God made him who had no sin to be sin for us, so that in him we might become the righteousness of God" (2 Cor. 5:21).

It might be well to gather up what we have covered so far, along with what is just ahead, in these three statements:

1. Adam's sin is imputed to us.
2. Our sin is imputed to our Redeemer.
3. Christ's righteousness is imputed to us.

Grasping these truths will effectively shut down pride and deliver us from assuming the impossible burden of trying to merit forgiveness. We are absolutely closed to all else but repenting for our sin and relying by faith on what Christ has done.

## A Lost Word—Propitiation

Turn again to Ephesians 5:2 and to figure 1. Meditate on the two arrows. The first, aimed Godward, designates what Christ does *in my place, in my stead, or in my behalf.* The second arrow, reaching to the kneeling figure, highlights what Christ does *in my life.* Confusing these two distinct works of Christ brings serious misunderstanding and error.

The grand biblical word for Christ's offering "to God" on our behalf is *propitiation.* It is much to be regretted that a term of such depth and importance has slipped from our understanding. Better than any other word, it expresses the original language and intent of Scripture. It carries the truth that our Savior's sacrifice to God is effective in satisfying God's justice (which we have offended) and restoring us to favor with the Father. It carries a glorious message to prisoners of sin!

When we believe in this Savior, the Lord Jesus Christ, then his propitiation offered to the Father becomes our payment for sin. Understanding propitiation opens salvation's door and sheds light on all that follows in our discussion.

What Jesus did *in our place* 2,000 years ago satisfies God's justice so perfectly that the Father then commences an ongoing work *in our lives.* These two works—that of justifying us and that of sanctifying us—must be distinguished but not separated. What Jesus does in our place is simply embraced by faith, whereas God's work in our lives mobilizes our volition and enables our concurrence, as we soon will see.

# 4

# God's Success Within

Pride changes coats quickly, almost unnoticed. When we are finally brought low by the gospel's insistence that our only hope of being right with God is through Christ's dying on the cross as payment for our sin, our pride still does not quit.

The monster of pride soon enough reappears, even in the preaching of the cross—in the teachings of those who present the blood's cleansing of the sinner as if that inward change were the foundation of the atonement. Do you see it? These teachers make the basis of the atonement its impact on the believer rather than its propitiation of the Father in heaven.

What pride is ours! First, we sinful beings presume to qualify ourselves before God, holding to our own merits. "No!" says the gospel preacher. "You cannot make yourselves right with God by self-effort." (And he is certainly right in this warning.) But then the same evangelist, who led the repentant away from trusting their own efforts at reformation, will by defective preaching lead them to rely instead on what Christ accomplishes in their hearts and lives. Despite this careless emphasis (a mixing of justification and sanctification), we not only are not saved by what we do for God, we also are not justified by what he does in us.

Please let me repeat. None are declared righteous on the basis of what Christ does in their lives. Believers are declared righteous only on the basis of what Christ offered up to God in our behalf 2,000 years ago. Salvation comes to the one who rests completely on what Jesus offered up to God on our behalf. That offering is the basis for the full salvation that is intended to deepen and flower in each believer's life.

Praise be to God that we are not declared righteous because of any changes within but because of what Jesus did in our place on the cross! Therefore that saving, justifying work is unchangeable, untouchable. Grasping this truth, a believer is no longer exposed to so many tormenting inner doubts and assaults by the Accuser.

## Deeper Yet

But we are not yet at the bottom of the matter. It is true, as we have just observed, that our eternal salvation does not rest on our goodness, or even on what good changes God might work within us. But what does it finally depend on? Underneath everything is the eternal plan of the holy and righteous God, who is love. He has planned from eternity the salvation of his people. He freely takes the initiative. We do not deserve or draw his mercy to us. Thus our salvation is "to the praise of his glorious grace, which he has freely given us in the One he loves" (Eph. 1:6), and the wondrous demonstration of this love is seen in the way God justly settles our debt of guilt.

Early in my pastoral experience, I discovered that fellow pastors could affirm their belief in Christ's propitiation and at the same time be confused about the ultimate basis of the sinner's reconciliation with God. This very topic arose in a discussion that occurred in a national missions committee on which I served. I had just stated my belief in Christ's propitiation of divine justice on our behalf. I heard no objections until I spoke of the need for God to be reconciled to the sinner. Then the conference table became all astir in a concerted effort to correct me. They were saying that God, in love, already was reconciled, in proof of which he gave his Son to die for us, and now all that remains is for sinners to be reconciled to God.

While I agreed that sinners need to be reconciled to God, I sought to win my case for the objective side of reconciliation by insisting that Scripture teaches that God so loved that he *gave*, not, God so loved that he *forgave*. Only the blood offering of Christ propitiating God (see fig. 1) allows God to make a just reconciliation with us sinners. Then we can kneel on the basis of Christ's sacrifice and beg that we might be reconciled with God. Our impasse was suddenly broken by the gruff words of a theology professor at the table, who sounded forth with his characteristic bluntness. "Back off, men! Burchett is right." The issue dropped there for most, but not for me. I still prize this truth.

## The Common Thread
Running through all we have covered so far in this chapter is the common thread of truth that our salvation is founded upon the objective work that Christ does in our behalf, not upon any subjective, inner changes in our lives. Thinking back to the threefold definition of sin, it will be apparent that once the legal issue of guilt is settled by the propitiation of Christ, then salvation can relieve the other two aspects of sin—our disposition toward sin, and its expression in the evil ways we think and act.

Let's take stock of where we now are.

1. The law no longer is after us; we have peace with God through Christ's blood sacrifice.
2. God takes us in and fathers us. We are born of his Spirit. We are children of God (1 John 3:1).

49

3. A major crisis, however, is bound to confront us, for evil desires yet lurk within us, perhaps nourished by years of practice. Waves of new joy soon break their crests on the hard rocks of this deeply embedded carnality.

Consistently, God orders us to quit sin, to be holy as he is holy. Rather consistently, however, we fail. Discouragement sets in. We know Christ died for us, but we perhaps experience little of his life within. Here is a text that will perhaps bring fresh, liberating insights: "How much more, then, will the blood of Christ, who through the eternal Spirit offered himself unblemished to God, cleanse our consciences from acts that lead to death, so that we may serve the living God!" (Heb. 9:14).

Great truth is plainly put here. The Savior's blood is an unblemished offering to God. This to-God offering produces priceless horizontal effects. New results appear in the life. The defiled conscience becomes pure. Deadly personal sins drop away, and God is served in actions and attitudes. Read the text carefully in the light of its context. Then consider this thought: If you harbor the least doubt about the value of Christ's sacrifice to satisfy God's just requirements, a painful toll will be exacted within your heart and life. Putting it in different words: Whenever the full settlement of all charges against us is not made clear to the heart by God's Spirit, faith will be contaminated by doubts and uncertainty. In such a condition, keeping confidence before God requires effort and strength we simply don't have. Repeated failure in sin will surely be the end result.

The effects of Christ's sacrifice that are mentioned in Hebrews 9:14 seem at once clear and much to be desired by us. But the text is saying more. We are being shown how this blood offering brings about these much-desired alterations within the believer's heart and life. It is this: Christ "through the eternal Spirit offered himself unblemished to God." The Father is propitiated, satisfied, and guilt is gone. The changes in us do not bring about this favor with God. Rather, the settlement our Savior makes with God results in these changes. It is so important to fight all battles against sin by standing on that foundation. Remember, "Without the shedding of blood there is no forgiveness" (Heb. 9:22). But now after the cross is embraced, full pardon is offered, and it is followed by the Spirit's entrance into the believing heart to begin the transformations of personal sanctification. Once sin's deep legal root is dealt with, we stand justified in Christ, and the Spirit begins his work in each cooperative heart to correct inner corruption and curb wrongdoing.

## A Quick and Crucial Overview and Preview

Standing at the headwaters of salvation's river is Jesus Christ and only he. Early in our studies, I pointed out that the name or title "Christ" is a one-word summation of the Bible. Also I cited passages in Colossians and elsewhere that assert that Christ is God the Son, the image of God, the reservoir of the fullness of God. Furthermore, he is Head of our lineage. Also we have seen that the biblical phrases "in Christ" and "in him," as well as related phrases like "with Christ" or "through Christ," form a virtual two-word key to so much of Scripture. This key truth is woven into the very warp and woof of the Epistles, whether expressed or implied.

Even with this key in hand, doors of truth will remain locked if the meaning of that concept is not fully understood. It means, first of all, as we have already said, that Christ stands in my place. But there is more. The conclusion must also be drawn that what he does as my Representative is considered as *my* act, as if

*I* did the thing that Jesus does in my name. Please hold in mind this position that Jesus assumes in my stead and my resulting identification with him because it will come up again shortly and will be a crucial point in our progress.

Partnering close with the truth that *I am in Christ* (or, Christ is standing in my place) is the companion teaching that *Christ is in me.* The former concept denotes a *legal* position, whereas the latter is *experiential.* Understanding the first and claiming it by faith leads to the second, which involves our practice.

The first half of Romans 6 expresses what Christ did in our stead 2,000 years ago and is now counted as true for us. But many Bible interpreters force these very words to apply instead to the concept of Christ in me, that is, to my spiritual experience. In this manner they lose hold of important teaching on my place in Christ and introduce confusion by bringing up how I am doing in my experience with Christ.

## The Great Divide—Where Many Jump Ship

It is one thing to call Christ our Substitute and Propitiation as we see how he provides for our right standing with God. It is quite another thing, though, to see how his work as our Representative is also foundational for all our cleansing and growth in sanctification. When faced with heart-rending personal struggles against evil desires, many are left drowning in confusion at the mixed messages they hear from those who teach the Scripture. Some teachers talk of justification as Christ's "part" and our growth and cleansing as "our part," with God's help. Without question, these teachers have abandoned the ship on which they began their journey.

Others have slipped quite unconsciously overboard into the same watery doctrine. They are like those Paul warned of who "do not know what they are talking about or what they so confidently affirm" (1 Tim. 1:7). Some people thrashing about in this water are recognized Bible expositors, along with large numbers of believers who began well enough but are now being hindered by "sound" Bible teaching.

### "Man (Woman) Overboard!"

Let's interview some of those splashing about in the waters of confusion.

Q: Did you not begin with an emphasis on what Jesus did in our stead?

A: Yes, I did.

Q: Then why have you left that foundation and now emphasize what the Savior accomplishes within us?

A: Because the former was "positional truth"; now we are talking about what is experienced in the life. *(puffs and gasps)*

Q: Are you not confusing Jesus' perfect offering to God with the application of that work to your heart and life? Little wonder your breathing is so labored! What the Spirit is accomplishing in you has *not* reached the perfection stated in the texts that speak of what Jesus did for us and of what we are in him. Faith cannot make the unreal real or make a fiction a fact. Please let me explain. Come back aboard, and let's discuss these truths.

Getting back aboard the Good Ship *Propitiation*, we can now examine the loose railing allowing the fatal slips overboard. To repeat, on the cross our Savior vicariously stands in for us, receiving our death-stroke of punishment for sin. Once we are declared fully pardoned by reason of our having been executed (via Christ) for all crimes, we must maintain this position *in our Representative*. We may now live a new life in holiness by standing in that relationship before God and claiming the Spirit's help.

## The Stark Difference between Teachers Still Onboard and Those in the Water

"If the Son sets you free, you will be free indeed" (John 8:36). We readily agree that the Son brings complete freedom, but are we experiencing it? Yes, we understand his release from charges of guilt, but what of the discouraging stranglehold of our sinful nature, with its lurking inner desires for evil—the anger, bitterness, lust, dishonesty, and materialistic greed? What are we to make of the humbling flashbacks from our former sinful life? No defeat is so painful as that which comes in spite of new light.

This struggle is universal, and three wrong ways open before us as we try to avoid painful spiritual lapses:

1. Live in a state of numb pride, denying the lively control of personal sin in our lives, while presuming that God's grace will flex enough to cover for us. *or*
2. Live with the dread that the Father in heaven will eventually bring down the chastening rod upon our disobedient backs, as Hebrews 12:5-11 teaches. *or*
3. Keep occupied with the popular teachings that give wishful assurance of personal triumph over sin's grip—though not based on Bible truth.

The third alternative above is often a collecting ground for large numbers of puzzled and disheartened people, so I will turn to that now. Because of the popularity of the positions we must unseat, I will take special care to show the right interpretations of key biblical texts.

Turn to the principal text on this subject, Romans 6–8. Look at these words, "We died to sin," from 6:2. Now let's ask questions of the text.

*According to Romans 6:2, what died?* It does not say my flesh or my sin nature or my sinful inclinations died. No "part" of me died. Instead, the text is simply informing us that *we* (believers) died.

*When did this death take place?* It happened in the past. It is not said to be in process or progress. No, we *died.* Please stay on board as we continue. Keep it firmly in mind that there is only one already-past-and-accomplished death that we believers are involved in—the death of Christ in our place. Calvary's death is *our* death in the full sense. We are counted as having died when our Substitute suffered in our stead.

*What kind of death is it?* It is death *to sin.* Here is the point where so many abandon ship. Review what has just been covered. Review also the three basic aspects of sin. Only one aspect fits with the context here, namely, sin as legal guilt. All our blame, or condemnation, was laid on—assigned to—the One who represented us. We are counted as having died because Jesus bore our guilt and died in regard to the charges that stood against us. God is telling us in this Scripture that, in his records, we have paid what our state of sin demanded—that is, death. This is the sense here of "We died to sin."

Spurious interpretations of this little text abound, leaving believers without the help they need. Those in painful struggle with personal sins are met with a barrage of conflicting views. Here are several examples of how the phrase "we died to sin" is misinterpreted.

*Example 1.* "We died to the pull of sin in our lives." First, notice that this interpretation is built on a totally wrong understanding of "sin," as the word is used in this portion of Scripture. Second, God surely is not announcing to Bible readers that they are dead to the pull of sin! A variation of this error promises that faith can be stretched to cover the apparent discrepancy between what is promised and what is experienced. "You just have to believe it, as God says it," the preacher or writer might say. But the truth is that we are not dead to sin in the way being taught, and faith cannot make something be that is not. Faith is not designed to breach the law of contradiction.

*Example 2.* "We died to the necessity of sin." This somewhat obscure statement is not utterly false in itself, but it redefines the words. Remember, "sin" in Romans 6:2 is speaking of our judicial guilt, and the words "died to" refer to the demanded execution for guilt. The guilty one must face and die to those charges. Jesus became our stand-in and assumed our condemnation: "God made him who had no sin to be sin for us, so that in him we might become the righteousness of God" (2 Cor. 5:21).

*Example 3.* "We died to our old sinful nature." First, that is not what the text says. Second, experience also disproves it.

*Example 4.* "Jesus does it all for us; we have only to believe." This view confuses what Jesus did in our stead with what he does in us. His judicial work as our dying Substitute brings justification and a perfect record in heaven. But our life on earth, which needs personal sanctification, is far from perfect. Belief, or faith, is indeed essential for both justification and sanctification, although its manner of operating in the two is very different. In the next chapter we examine this difference more thoroughly.

*Example 5.* "Death" is interpreted so as not to have a literal, physical meaning. But the death that is ours (assigned to us, counted as ours) is the death that Jesus died—a very literal and physical one. This death of Jesus in our place must be kept in view throughout, or the passage will be clouded with serious error.

## The Correct Understanding of Romans 6:2

Examine Romans 6:1-2 carefully, making very sure that you are not superimposing on the phrases what you so often have heard, rather than understanding what the words are really saying. Notice, first of all, that we are not being told that sin is now beyond us, or that we won't have the urge to sin. But we are told in strong terms that it is unthinkable that we should choose such a way, in the light of our vicarious execution. Also be aware that the plural term "sins," or the third aspect of sin, is not being spoken of here. Rather, the text considers our state of legal condemnation before God.

## Proof from the Context

Verses from the first half of Romans 6 clearly support the interpretation we are setting forth. To recap: (1) Christ's crucifixion was an execution for sin; (2) his death is counted by God as our own death; and (3) the death we died was thus carried out by proxy, in our stead, by a substitute. This is the death being spoken of in verse 2 and following. (This passage simply continues the theme of the previous chapter. Romans 5 shows how we stand in our Representative, Jesus Christ, just as we once stood in Adam. Whereas Adam brought condemnation and death, Christ brings justification and life.) Now, let's continue on down through chapter 6.

*Verse 3.* Baptism portrays the believer's inclusion in the Lord's death. Jesus' death is a penal one. He is paying for our sin.

*Verse 7.* Move past verse 6 for the moment and study very carefully the words of this brief portion: "Anyone who has died has been freed from sin." Notice that most popular translations are very nonspecific in using the term "freed." However, the Greek word here translated "freed" (from sin), a term used frequently by Paul, is elsewhere taken to mean "acquitted" or "justified." Whatever this dying entails, it leads to our legal release from all God's charges against us. Only our death via the Savior brings our acquittal! Freedom from overpowering urges of sin is not being spoken of in this portion of Romans 6. Rather, we died in Jesus to the legal charges against us—that is the theme here, as in verse 2. Verse 8 joins in to make clear that Paul is referring to our death "with Christ."

*Verse 10.* Surely this verse should settle the matter: "The death he died, he died to sin once for all." The death being spoken of throughout our passage is a judicial one. The Lord Jesus Christ is sinless and thus did not go through any experience of putting to death inner sinful urges. Rather, he "died to sin" as he faced the charges laid on him on our account, in our stead.

*Verse 11.* "In the same way, count yourselves dead to sin but alive to God in Christ Jesus." We are told here to count Jesus' death on Calvary as our own execution to sin's legal charges. God has indeed credited Christ's redemptive work to us, but we must count it as truly ours. This understanding is the basis for releasing new life within us.

## Proof from Other Scriptures

Notice the same line of thought in other passages. Consider, for example, Colossians 3:3: "For you died, and your life is now hidden with Christ in God." What died? No part of me. Nor can I say that desires for sin have ceased. Simply, "I died." The only sense in which that is true is in Christ Jesus. I died with him, or through him, as my Representative. When did this dying occur? The past, completed tense here makes it clear that it was when

Jesus died, 2,000 years ago.

In verse 5 we are ordered to decisively put down sinful expressions of our earthly nature. The word "therefore" indicates that this putting down is to be done in the light of—on the basis of—what has just been mentioned.

Notice a similar expression of Christ's death in our stead as the basis for our response: "For Christ's love compels us, because we are convinced that one died for all, and therefore all died" (2 Cor. 5:14). Look carefully at the verse's central statement, "we are convinced that one died for all." Understand that the apostle is sharing with us a life-changing conviction that our Savior's death was an intentional sacrifice in behalf of "all."

Now see how this transforming central conviction is connected with the words before it and with what follows. Christ's love grips us "because we are convinced" of this central truth. And this truth of the Lord's representing us on the cross "therefore" leads to the wondrous result that "all died." I say wondrous, because that death is graciously attributed to us as payment for our sin.

## Try It: Going from Effect back to Cause in Romans 6:6

Let us return now to Romans 6 for a study of verse 6:

> For we know that our old self was crucified with him
> so that the body of sin might be done away with,
> that we should no longer be slaves to sin.

Helpful insights can be drawn from this text if we move from the last clause (which is an effect or result) to the middle clause (the cause of that particular effect), and then likewise from the middle clause back to the first.

The words "that we should no longer be slaves to sin" are presented to us as the very desirable result of the words just preceding, "the body of sin . . . done away with." Here is the meaning: when our sinful nature is given an incapacitating blow, sin's enslaving chains are broken off.

Going further with the verse, we see that the cause of this liberation is itself a result of the clause just preceding it. Study each cause and effect carefully, remembering that we are moving in reverse. The words "so that" indicate that what has just been stated produces the knock-out punch to the controlling sinful nature, and that action in turn releases us from slavery to sin. What is the delivering truth that sets all this change in motion? "Our old self was crucified with him." That is it!

Please don't leave the solid ground established here. Remember two things: (1) the phrase "body of sin" stands for the "flesh," or sinful nature; (2) that which was crucified "with him" was not some part of us. Rather, "we" died with him. When he died, I died. Therefore the Greek expression here translated "our old self" means the one we were in our old (lost, unsaved) life. The one I was in my sinful state—that one—God executed via my Substitute on Calvary's cross.

Notice further that all this spiritual sequence is set in motion with the opening words, "For we know that. . . ." Paul is saying in verse 6 that the deep identification of the believer with Jesus, spoken of in the chapter's opening verses, is understandable truth. We are assured that the sinful person we were, in our old life, was justly executed with Jesus so that the oppressive tendency to sin might lose its stranglehold, in order that, finally, we should no longer be compelled to sin.

With this loose paraphrase of verse 6 before you, carefully and prayerfully review it together with the Bible text until all is clear.

## Don't Forget the Key!
I have already referred to the phrase "in Christ" or "in him" as

being a key to Scripture and its whole scheme of salvation. To get at all our advantages in grace, we must see the full meaning of this truth. First, it has to do with our inclusion in Jesus Christ as he positioned himself as the "last Adam" (1 Cor. 15:45) and endured the judgment stroke due Adam and all his progeny.

Then Jesus rose from the grave as the "second man" (1 Cor. 15:47), and as such he heads a new lineage. Having escaped Adam's headship, the believer is now related to Jesus Christ as Head. Countless new family privileges are waiting. These privileges, though, are all from a position that must be understood and applied in faith.

Look again at 2 Corinthians 5:14-15: "For Christ's love compels us, because we are convinced that one died for all, and therefore all died. And he died for all, that those who live should no longer live for themselves but for him who died for them and was raised again." Jesus' death for "all" was (1) to count for "all" believers, so that it may be considered that we all died when he died, and (2) to bring us into new life.

Rarely have I heard any comments on what immediately follows. However, when verse 16 is given its proper place, then the popular interpretations of verse 17 are suspect. The first words of each verse demand their close connection. Keeping in mind verses 14 and 15, consider also the next two verses:

> [16]So from now on we regard no one from a worldly point of view. Though we once regarded Christ in this way, we do so no longer. [17]Therefore, if anyone is in Christ, he is a new creation; the old has gone, the new has come!

Verse 16 teaches us that there are two very different ways of looking at humanity. We can view them naturally, as a single mass of world population. Or we can see them with spiritual eyes, as divided into two groups: those who are in Adam and those who are in Christ, or those who are in the family of Adam and those in the family of Christ. This fundamental distinction, which is established in verses 14 and 15, must determine the way we look at our Head, Jesus Christ, and those who are his. Sadly, it must be admitted that many believers go happily on their way with little thought of this way of looking at mankind.

Evidence of this weak, shallow look at reality is close at hand. Just replay in your mind the teachings you have heard from the popular verse 17, remembering that just as the word "so" in 16 connects it back to verses 14 and 15, so "therefore" in 17 relates it to verse 16. Follow this reasoning carefully and you will see that 17 cannot be referring to the expression of our new nature as believers. All too obviously the sin nature has *not* gone. The only fully accomplished fact is that *in Christ* we are of a new order of creation. The Second Man is our Head. Our lineage has changed. Out of Adam and into Christ. Guilt is gone! This is the message Christ's ambassadors are commissioned to proclaim, according to the verses that follow. And the last verse of the chapter locks the passage into this interpretation. What we are *in Christ* is the foundational truth being established here. Don't forget this key!

Second Corinthians 5:17 itself hands us this very key by opening with the words "if anyone is in Christ"—not "if Christ is in anyone." Our inner changes when Christ begins his work *in us* is another matter, and it is the theme to which we now turn.

# 5

# NEW LIFE—WITHOUT
# SHACKLES OF SIN

All human beings who lack salvation in Christ are under
the sentence of death, along with their father Adam. This
death displays itself from conception in each life—first as an
inner defilement of character, or a nature of sin, and next as the
physical loss of life. On the intake side, our sinful nature opens
the senses to all manner of temptation. On the output side, what
the Scripture calls the acts, desires, or cravings of the sinful nature
bring an enslavement to the practice of sin. Evil desires, attitudes,
actions, and words tend toward habituation, leading to shackles
of enslavement.

Rancorous thoughts rumble about deep down in the typical
heart. Lusts and cravings simmer there, molding and misshaping
the character and direction of life. Much of this smoldering may
be unnoticed by friends and family at first, but these infections
eventually break out on the skin of things, to the shock of those
around and perhaps to the chagrin of the one hosting the unholy
heart.

## After-Birth Discouragement

The acts and attitudes of the sinful nature are quite native to the one who is an unregenerate person. But those who have truly surrendered to, and believed in, the Lord Jesus Christ are given the Spirit of God to help them walk a new way.

Repeatedly in Scripture we are taught that those in their natural state as part of Adam's family cannot live pleasing to God. The same Word, though, shines with encouragement to believers. To them, Jesus says, "If the Son sets you free, you will be free indeed" (John 8:36). But many believers do not experience true freedom.

Here, then, is the single most poignant and, in a way, utterly impossible problem that each Christian must solve. How can I do and be what I ought? Even after entering the way of salvation, I keep stumbling, and in some ways sin hassles me more than before. Telling me that all this struggle is "common to man" (1 Cor. 10:13) further discourages me. Surely Jesus died to accomplish something better than this! In addition, trusted Bible teachers keep assuring me that I have a new "deadness" to sin, if I would only believe it. Something is wrong in that teaching, for I actually feel a new sensitivity and pull toward sin.

## Precisely What Is This New Freedom?

Our new release from the dominion of sin is twofold. First, we were executed 2,000 years ago for, or with reference to, all charges of guilt through our Substitute and Representative, Jesus Christ (Rom. 6:2; Col. 3:3). Believers are thus acquitted, legally freed, or justified, as Romans 6:7 assures us. Judgment is over, forever settled. We are permanently released from the charges of sin. Guilt is gone.

Second, the One who satisfied the Judge on our behalf now comes to live within our hearts by the Holy Spirit and bring us into new freedom in our living.

We stand now at the crisis point. Three sources of troubling distress keep earnest believers swamped in confusion regarding the Christian's freedom from sin:

1. Our self-centered concerns about sin focus on what troubles *us* about sin, not on how *God* is offended.

2. Satan's wily accusations cause us to look so much at our imperfect performance that we lose sight of what Jesus did in our stead and what the Holy Spirit waits to do in our lives.

3. Well-meaning Bible teachers pull the foundation from beneath the feet of struggling believers by taking Scriptures that speak of Jesus' death on Calvary, in my stead, and improperly applying them to my present experience. (Remember: When Scripture says "I died" or "we died," it is talking of Calvary, where believers died in their Substitute, not about my experience.)

If we consider the two dimensions of salvation—what Christ does in our place, and then what he does in our life—it should be apparent that the second concept is founded upon the first. Once God is propitiated, satisfied, he stands ready to grant us a gracious assistance in our battle to quit sinning and begin loving God and others as we should.

The resulting freedom is not founded in the imagined death of the old nature, nor should it be defined vaguely as the death of "the old nature's claims." No, our Father, who is satisfied with our death in Christ, is now free to deal with us in loving-kindness as his very own children. For the first time we have the freedom *not* to sin.

## The Option of Not Sinning

At this point, believers divide into two groups. Some grasp for freedom from wrong desires and urges as a kind of all-done gift. (Invariably, these believers will bow sooner or later in discouraging defeat.) Much better off are those who stand on their release from guilt and their new favor with God—through Christ's sacrifice—and, in bold faith, claim the Holy Spirit's help to put down sin in their heart and practice. Though this help is not automatically pressed into our lives, all we need is available to faith: "His divine power has given us everything we need for life and godliness through our knowledge of him who called us by his own glory and goodness" (2 Peter 1:3).

The provision of "everything we need for life and godliness" comes to us in the gift of the Holy Spirit. Turn to Romans 8, and observe in the opening verses that our being "in Christ Jesus" is shown to be foundational to all that follows. Each child of God is said to have the Spirit, who stands ready to bring the new dimension of release from sin's control.

As Jesus Christ's death frees us from condemnation, so the Holy Spirit enters our lives to help in breaking the control of sin in our lives. Think carefully about the distinction between our being in Christ and his indwelling us. The two expressions "in him" and "he in us" are inseparable, but they are not identical. Believers are counted "in him" as Jesus received the judgment stroke for sin that is due us. Next, his work "in us" is accomplished by the Spirit.

Again, notice carefully the distinction between the works of justification and sanctification. The former, Jesus did in our behalf, in our place, 2,000 years ago. In contrast, the latter is the work of the Spirit and occurs day by day, always with our full involvement. The Spirit works *in* us, in concurrence with our wills. Thus, through the Spirit, we have the option not to sin. (The Spirit does much more, as Romans 8 teaches.)

We are never ordered to work for the forgiveness of our sins. No, Christ does that as a free gift for us. Then we are commanded to quit sin. But how? Failure now enters the picture and overwhelms us—until we learn how to cooperate by faith and choose to concur with the gracious ministry of the Spirit and then to live in the strength of divine enablement.

## Focusing on the Problem That Squeezes Out Christ

Losing sight of the twofold nature of grace perverts both doctrine and practice. Imagine the frustration of the faithful trying to practice what is promised, and then trying to accept by faith what is commanded. This confusion arises from the misrepresentations of Scripture pointed out in the previous pages. When teachers explain those texts without making it clear whether God is simply *informing* us of something or is *ordering* and *obligating* us to a certain response, they pull their listeners overboard into waters of confusion.

When God says "you died," we are being informed about something that has been accomplished. Look again at Colossians 3:3. Notice the word "therefore" in verse 5, which accompanies the stark command "put to death!" "Therefore" makes the essential connection between this obligation to deal decisively with ("put to death") things of the earthly nature with what has already occurred in verse 3 and, according to verse 4, will one day be gloriously completed.

In grace, God provides our right standing with him, and in grace he grants us the Holy Spirit's help to do whatever he obligates us to do. Here is the twofold nature of grace—Christ doing in our stead what we could never do, and then Christ coming alongside us and within us to enable us to respond to the call to holiness. Remember: these two dimensions of grace must always be distinguished but never separated. Later, in part 2, where we focus on counseling and discipling and other vital practices of our faith, it will become very clear what great harm is done in misapplying these truths.

## Missing the Resurrection While Defending It

We have not yet stressed the resurrection of our Lord, but the time has come to do so. That Jesus arose from the grave is a historical fact. It is possible, though, to proclaim this fact from the narrative accounts in the Gospels and from Acts and yet to omit great truths that the Epistles associate with our Lord's resurrection. A primary power loss occurs right at this point.

We can well agree with the apostle Paul in 1 Corinthians 15 that if Christ has not been raised from the dead, our preaching is in vain, we are yet in our sins, and we are much to be pitied. On the positive side, we delight to hear Jesus' words, "I am the resurrection and the life," with its accompanying promise that those who believe in him will live eternally (John 11:25-26). Like water from the well in an oasis, a stream of other truths rises from the Lord's resurrection. All his earlier ministry and sacrificial death are vindicated as the Father raises him to life. Not only vindicated, but his great work is, by the resurrection, continued on earth and in heaven and extended into a glorious future.

What often is missed, however, is the representative nature of his rising to new life. From the womb, Jesus came into our world of humanity and went into death bearing our judgment. As the Last Adam, our Stand-in paid all our sin-debt and prepared the way for us to begin a new life with him before God. In his life, no less than in his death, we are with our Savior, just as Romans

6:8 teaches: "Now if we died *with* Christ, we believe that we will also live *with* him."

Consider carefully the key preposition "with." We are not being told here that Christ is *with us* in fellowship. No, *we* are said to be *with him*. In what way? Not physically, but in our identification with him as our official Substitute or Representative. As Jesus dies and rises from death, his actions are credited to us; we are identified *with him* in what he did. God counts it that way, and our salvation depends on these vital facts.

## The Crown Rescued from the Mud

I doubt that many of us see with full understanding either the heights to which Adam and Eve were commissioned or the depths to which they fell, since one gives the measure of the other. They were made in God's image and crowned as head over creation. The writer of Hebrews quotes from Psalm 8 and then goes wide-screen for his dramatic presentation of these momentous scenes:

> "What is man that you are mindful of him, the son of man that you care for him? You made him a little lower than the angels; you crowned him with glory and honor and put everything under his feet."
>
> In putting everything under him, God left nothing that is not subject to him. Yet at present we do not see everything subject to him. But we see Jesus, who was made a little lower than the angels, now crowned with glory and honor because he suffered death, so that by the grace of God he might taste death for everyone.
>
> In bringing many sons to glory, it was fitting that God, for whom and through whom everything exists, should make the author of their salvation perfect through suffering. Both the one who makes men holy and those who are made holy are of the same family. So Jesus is not ashamed to call them brothers. (Heb. 2:6-11)

Focus the camera of your imagination on mankind's once-glorious crown. See it lie sunken in the mire of sinful degradation, as described in Genesis. Now splice in a couple more poignant scenes. First, God in anguish looks over the world of Noah's day:

> The LORD saw how great man's wickedness on the earth had become, and that every inclination of the thoughts of his heart was only evil all the time. The LORD was grieved that he had made man on the earth, and his heart was filled with pain. So the LORD said, "I will wipe mankind, whom I have created, from the face of the earth—men and animals, and creatures that move along the ground, and birds of the air—for I am grieved that I have made them." (Gen. 6:5-7)

We mourn with the prophet Jeremiah as he confesses, "The crown has fallen from our head. Woe to us, for we have sinned!" (Lam. 5:16).

In the second scene of our viewing, many centuries later, God again speaks—this time of Jesus: "This is my Son, whom I love; with him I am well pleased" (Matt. 3:17). At last the Father has unrestrained pleasure, in this One who is his own.

Now let us see how we fit into the picture. Turning again to the Hebrews 2 segment, we hear that the rulership lost by us humans has been assumed by Jesus Christ: "We see Jesus, who was made a little lower than the angels, now crowned with glory and honor" (v. 9). The crown we lost now shines in splendor on his brow.

But before the glory, Jesus came forth from Mary's womb, born in our broken likeness (Rom. 8:3) to stand in our place and receive our punishment for sin. He bears our shame on the cross and into the grave. Next, we see him issuing from the tomb, born as the Second Man, "the firstborn from among the dead, so that in everything he might have the supremacy" (Col. 1:18). Here he is not joining us in our misery; rather, he is making a way for us to rise with him into eternal glory.

To know what our new state is like, we have only to remember that we have believed *into* Christ. This means that we may by faith view his rising in new life and his entering glory as including us. Since he acts on our behalf, we are *in* him and *with* him, as God counts things. "Just as Christ was raised from the dead through the glory of the Father, we too may live a new life" (Rom. 6:4). We may—and must—claim by faith what is ours in Christ Jesus.

## The Womb and the Tomb

From the womb Jesus came forth to go to the cross. From the tomb Jesus came forth to go to the throne. Since he is, throughout all this way, on assignment to represent us personally, we are said to be "with him" in all this. He first takes our name and guilt so that we may then, after inauguration into new life, take his name and righteousness. Putting it in other words, Jesus came from the womb to join our fallen family and gain our release from Adam's lineage. He comes from the tomb to invite us to join his new family, of which he is Head. "If we have been united with him like this in his death, we will certainly also be united with him in his resurrection" (Rom. 6:5).

Things joined inseparably may still be distinguished—such as the effects and benefits of the cross and of the resurrection. God counts me with and in Christ as my penalty is exacted from him as my Substitute. His cross makes a full legal, or judicial, settlement and therefore provides just grounds for God to include me in the resurrection. I am "with Christ" as he rises. Nor is this union left as a mere matter of record, or accounting. No, the Holy Spirit makes it real in my experience, so that, "just as Christ was raised from the dead through the glory of the Father, we too

71

may live a new life" (Rom. 6:4).

Those who call for a deeper spiritual life, as well as a release from the nag and drag of sinful desires, are in error if they do not put the resurrection of Christ in its proper place. The cross pays all the charges against me as a guilty sinner. God then includes his child in the new life with Christ. We do not have to imagine or "claim by faith" an illusory deadness to sin. Resurrection life in Christ with its new strength to overcome sinful allurements and urges is given to us. The Holy Spirit enters our hearts, and for the first time we may claim our freedom not to sin. The Spirit personally works to strengthen my volition, enabling me to "put to death the misdeeds of the body" and to live anew (Rom. 8:13). The first half of Romans 6 and the opening half of chapter 8 teach us to claim benefits of both the cross and the resurrection. To treat the latter as a mere add-on is to abandon ship at the very entrance to the harbor.

In this light, Galatians 2:20 should ring with new appeal: "I have been crucified with Christ and I no longer live, but Christ [the Resurrected One] lives in me. The life I live in the body, I live by faith in the Son of God, who loved me and gave himself for me."

## Between the Gallows and the Mansion

As we approach the final chapter of part 1 of this book, I know some will still be puzzling over the last words of Romans 6:2, "How can we live in it [sin] any longer?" The key is that Paul is not saying here that, for a Christian, sinning *can't be done;* rather, he is saying that it *surely ought not to be done.* If I may borrow your imagination for a moment, consider the following illustration.

Suppose that a young man's crimes have caught up with him,

and now he is being dragged into the village courthouse for trial. An angry crowd jams the sidewalk, crying for his blood. The youth's fears turn to utter panic when he sees that a scaffold has already been erected on the green beside the courthouse.

Inside, a serious-faced judge confronts him with the charges, which deserve the death sentence. The guilty man staggers as he is sentenced to die on the gallows.

But suddenly the judge points toward the window, crying out, "But there's my son . . . and it's for you!" One look sends the shock of truth through the youth's being. There hanging from the scaffold is the judge's only son; the innocent has died for the guilty. The amazed man struggles to take it all in: "The judge's son dies for me?!"

But there's more. The magistrate steps from behind his bench and in tenderest love wraps strong arms about the staggered, now weeping, youth. Together they walk to the courthouse door to face the mob outside. Stunned silence! The guilty, in the arms of the judge! In a few words, the judge gives his astonishing explanation. "My son died on the gallows there in place of this one, who is therefore forgiven. And now I take the young man home with me, adopting him as my son!" The rabble fall back as the two walk through their midst, heading home to the judge's own mansion. (See Rom. 3:25-26.)

After an introduction to his beautiful new home on a hill outside of town, the youth, dressed in new clothing and now in his right mind, goes for an evening walk down to the village green. From the shadows of familiar haunts, voices of his past evil associates call out, beckoning him to return to the old sins.

He stands there on the village green—where we've all stood. On the one side, the seductive haunts are calling, urging, inviting. But high on the hill is the mansion of love. Lights in his own room send out their appeal for his return. Close by, in plain view, stands the gallows with its dangling cord—the very noose slung for his own neck but taken by the innocent substitute. Return to sin, in sight of the scaffolding?

Let all believers join the tempted youth in resolute chorus: *By no means! We died to sin; how can we live in it any longer?* (Rom. 6:2). Now that I have answered to all the charges against me by the death penalty (paid by the One who stood in for me), how can I turn back into the very evil from which I've escaped through such a costly arrangement? Rather, I now surrender willingly to the Holy Spirit. May he have his way in my life!

Without doubt, countless Christians long to bring back better days in their own personal experience, or perhaps to see new evidence of the Father's love and fidelity in their troubled world. What we really need, however, is to bring Christ back. My judgment is that the thoughtless imprecision in expressing the truths we are discussing has indeed squeezed our Lord into a kind of withdrawal. Where light is not, dark is—always. Fighting the dark is futile. Give thought and energy, instead, to returning the light.

When believers beg the Father in heaven for insight into these truths, surely our Savior is made glad. As comprehension comes, we must appropriate everything by prayer, making specific claims for grace and help and then living in the new light that God gives.

# 6

# WELCOME INTO
# GLORY—NOW!

It is appalling that we on earth have so little knowledge or concern about our Lord's messianic work in heaven when so much is revealed about it in Scripture. Yes, in God's Word the future return of Christ and our eternal home with him are made vividly real as our hope. But how sad it is if we stand on our little tiptoes, straining to figure out what the future holds, all the while overlooking what Jesus is doing in glory right now!

The One appointed as Mediator between God and men is at this very moment fulfilling this role in a very special manner. For a time, he was humbled beneath angels, obeyed parents, paid taxes, washed disciples' feet, and took our very sin on himself and died on the cross, paying our penalty for sin. Facing death, he said simply, "I came from the Father and entered the world; now I am leaving the world and going back to the Father" (John 16:28). Though now with the Father, he seamlessly maintains his alliance with us as begun on earth.

What is the full meaning of Jesus' pledge to remain with, and not leave, his disciples, even though he was returning to heaven? He no doubt had in mind the coming of the Spirit, and when he promised in the final sentence of Matthew, "I am with you always" (28:20), I think he also was indicating that he will never withdraw from headship of the human family. The name "Jesus" is very familiar in realms beyond earth. What ministries vital to us is the Lord Jesus Christ now performing in heaven? These glories are open for our delight and profit.

Because of the magnitude of the matters just before us, an advance look at an outline of the subject matter might prove helpful. Keep in mind these progressive points:

*First:* Jesus receives what is now his.

*Second:* What is his, now becomes ours.

*Third:* We now have four heavenly benefits.

### *First:* Jesus receives what is now his.

Jesus Christ "has gone into heaven and is at God's right hand—with angels, authorities and powers in submission to him" (1 Peter 3:22). His prayer of John 17:5 is now being answered: "And now, Father, glorify me in your presence with the glory I had with you before the world began."

These words do not mean that our Lord has abandoned his relationship with us. No, the Son did not stop being God or lay aside his deity when he came humbly into our world. Likewise, he did not stop being man and lay aside his humanity when he returned triumphantly into heaven. It is in this nature that he now reigns. And this reign continues until God "has put all his enemies under his feet" (1 Cor. 15:25). The incarnation, crucifixion, resurrection, ascension, and session at the Father's right hand have brought the glorious coronation of Christ. Furthermore, the glory and welcome to heaven accorded Jesus as Mediator have significance and reference to us.

### "Our Lord"

The confession that Jesus Christ is "our Lord" needs fresh

exploration. Since Jesus ascended to the throne in heaven, the title "Lord" rings with deeper tones. We miss much enriching insight by simply equating "Lord" and "God." While the Scripture might often use the two terms interchangeably, they are not identical, as applied to Christ. As Peter on Pentecost preaches, "God has made this Jesus, whom you crucified, both Lord and Christ" (Acts 2:36). Compare this wording with Paul's assertion that by his resurrection, Jesus Christ our Lord is "declared with power to be the Son of God" (Rom. 1:4). Or again, Thomas's confession, "My Lord and my God!" (John 20:28), where the disciple used two distinct terms.

While on earth Jesus said in the plainest of terms, "All things have been committed to me by my Father" (Matt. 11:27), and "as the Father has life in himself, so he has granted the Son to have life in himself. And he has given him authority to judge because he is the Son of Man" (John 5:26-27).

Acknowledging the Son's place in the Trinity is not all there is to it. We must understand that this one who has taken on humanity and paid for our sins through death on the cross now occupies the throne of the universe, and he is "the ruler of the kings of the earth" (Rev. 1:5). An unbelieving world rejected and crucified the Savior, but "God exalted him to the highest place and gave him the name that is above every name, that at the name of Jesus every knee should bow, in heaven and on earth and under the earth, and every tongue confess that Jesus Christ is Lord, to the glory of God the Father" (Phil. 2:9-11).

Surely, then, each one who is God's own child will respond to Peter's admonition, "In your hearts set apart Christ as Lord" (1 Peter 3:15). He is indeed *my* Lord!

## *Second:* What is his, now becomes ours.

Jesus' glory is our glory. Scripture says so. It also teaches us how his glory becomes ours. The Father works to make real our royalty.

Here is a magnificent Scripture that traces our Savior's history all the way from the recesses of the tomb to the glories at God's right hand in heaven. Furthermore, it spells out the place of believers with him there.

> I keep asking that the God of our Lord Jesus Christ, the glorious Father, may give you the Spirit of wisdom and revelation, so that you may know him better. I pray also that the eyes of your heart may be enlightened in order that you may know the hope to which he has called you, the riches of his glorious inheritance in the saints, and his incomparably great power for us who believe. That power is like the working of his mighty strength, which he exerted in Christ when he raised him from the dead and seated him at his right hand in the heavenly realms, far above all rule and authority, power and dominion, and every title that can be given, not only in the present age but also in the one to come. And God placed all things under his feet and appointed him to be head over everything for the church, which is his body, the fullness of him who fills everything in every way.
>
> As for you, you were dead in your transgressions and sins, in which you used to live when you followed the ways of this world and of the ruler of the kingdom of the air, the spirit who is now at work in those who are disobedient. All of us also lived among them at one time, gratifying the cravings of our sinful nature and following its desires and thoughts. Like the rest, we were by nature objects of wrath. But because of his great love for us, God, who is rich in mercy, made us alive with Christ even when we were dead in transgressions—it is by grace you have been saved. And God raised us up with Christ and seated us with him in

the heavenly realms in Christ Jesus, in order that in the coming ages he might show the incomparable riches of his grace, expressed in his kindness to us in Christ Jesus. (Eph. 1:17–2:7)

Review this sublime text, being careful to notice that the victories and glories of Jesus are being certified as our hope, and "his incomparably great power" is "for us who believe." Next, the delineation of all his sovereign glories culminates in the revelation that he is appointed "to be head over everything for the church, which is his body, the fullness of him who fills everything in every way." Our Savior is still *for us.*

Suddenly, in the second paragraph, the text drops us from the brilliance of heaven to the gloom of the tomb—our spiritual grave. It is a dark picture. Then the God who brought Jesus to life is said to raise us up with him and seat us "with him in the heavenly realms."

Surely these glorious truths should thrill our souls and lift us heavenward! Why do we seem more entombed than enthroned? A very large, hindering problem is our failure to understand how these realities are truly ours, not just our Lord's. Briefly review 1 Corinthians 15. What do you see in this large and important chapter? Study it carefully. At once you will see Paul's great defense of the literal, bodily resurrection of Jesus. Next, we view the ending of death's domination and the establishment of God's rule. The heavenly form of our own eternal existence is set forth also. But how are we tied into all that? This is the point we are now examining—what is his, now becomes ours.

To get at the answer, Paul refers us to Adam and our connection with him. "For as in Adam all die, so in Christ all will be made alive" (1 Cor. 15:22). Do you picture Jesus in heaven on your behalf? "And just as we have borne the likeness of the

earthly man, so shall we bear the likeness of the man from heaven"
(v. 49). Jesus' work as our Messiah and official Representative did
not end on earth. He rose with his body in a glorified condition,
but he has not left the human family. The death he died while
he was on earth is our payment for sin's guilt, to be claimed by
faith. But also his resurrection must be embraced by faith as our
release in this present life from the ravages of sin and death. In
none of these matters were we "there" instead of him. No, he
was there in our stead. That redeeming relationship continues.
We are not yet, in actual body experience, there in the heavens,
but he is there in our behalf in such a way that we may by faith
say, "God raised us up with Christ and seated us with him in the
heavenly realms" (Eph. 2:6). "Praise be to the God and Father of
our Lord Jesus Christ, who has blessed us in the heavenly realms
with every spiritual blessing in Christ" (Eph. 1:3)!

### *Third:* We now have four heavenly benefits.

These certainties must not seem to us as only "teachings about
Jesus." No, this is *our* history, being now restored to us. Let us
here make at least a partial inventory of our heavenly treasures.
We shall occupy ourselves with four of these benefits, giving
extended time to the first one:

1. Christ here with us, through the Holy Spirit
2. Christ there for us, making intercession
3. We here for Christ—his ambassadors
4. We together with him forever—our hope.

As we begin, we must admit that faith's knees tend to
buckle under the weight of these realities of heaven. We feel so
far removed from them all! We still struggle with sinful desires
within and agitations from without. How does the Father in
heaven propose to get the quickening impulse of Christ's new life

80

to operate within us? What is God's way of getting heaven into us, and one day getting us into heaven? These four truths provide the answers.

## 1. Christ Here with Us, through the Holy Spirit.

Solemnly, tenderly, Jesus promised in his last teachings before Calvary, "I will not leave you as orphans; I will come to you" (John 14:18). The Lord who "made his dwelling *among* us" (John 1:14) now is prepared to dwell *within* us by the Holy Spirit. The apostle Paul properly links these two "comings" in Galatians 4:4 and 6: "But when the time had fully come, God sent his Son, born of a woman" and "Because you are sons, God sent the Spirit of his Son into our hearts."

Peter's Pentecost message made this point: "God has raised this Jesus to life, and we are all witnesses of the fact. Exalted to the right hand of God, he has received from the Father the promised Holy Spirit and has poured out what you now see and hear" (Acts 2:32-33). As surely as Christ is *there,* the Spirit is *here,* just as our Lord promised: "If I go, I will send him to you" (John 16:8).

Since Adam's ignominious ouster from Eden, mankind's fellowship with God has been spotty at best, but now God has committed the dispensation of the Spirit into the hands of our Representative in heaven. As the Anointed One, he baptizes his own in the Holy Spirit. God is therefore prepared to walk with us in the garden of our hearts as his Spirit indwells us. By the Spirit "we may understand what God has freely given us" (1 Cor. 2:12).

Indeed, the coming of the Holy Spirit opens a new ministry *to* the hearts of unbelievers, as well as a new ministry *in* the hearts of believers. See this truth expressed clearly in John 16: "He will convict the world of guilt" (v. 8), and "He will guide you into all truth" (v. 13).

First, let's rehearse at least a portion of the Spirit's gracious work among believers before we review the works he performs among the unbelieving people of the world. The Spirit's ministry is really a continuation of Jesus' own life and working among believers, in a remarkably new form. Let us revel in the wonder of the following words spoken to the disciples as Jesus readied them for the soon coming of the Spirit (all in John 14):

> But you know him, for he lives with you and will be in you. (v. 17)

> He who loves me will be loved by my Father, and I too will love him and show myself to him. (v. 21)

> If anyone loves me, he will obey my teaching. My Father will love him, and we will come to him and make our home with him. (v. 23)

> All this I have spoken while still with you. But the Counselor, the Holy Spirit, whom the Father will send in my name, will teach you all things and will remind you of everything I have said to you. (vv. 25-26)

The works of the Spirit delineated in the Scripture are vast and varied as he works within and alongside God's children. For now, let us return to one ministry—his work in applying and making effective what Christ has provided in our behalf by his death and resurrection.

## The Man with Something Missing

Jake was high up in the military—and heated in his disposition. Sometimes I pitied Elizabeth, his soft-spoken and gracious wife. (Here and throughout the book, all names have been changed.)

But he was active in our church and seemed to know the Scripture well. In our weekly discipling sessions, he and I came to the subject of the Holy Spirit's work within a believer's life.

"Do you think of the Holy Spirit as a person?" I asked Jake.

After a long pause: "Well, not like you or me, but . . . uh . . . now, let's see . . . there is Father, Son, and Holy Spirit. But you are asking how I conceive of the Spirit. *(long pause)* No, I do not think of the Spirit that way—as a personal being. Yet, he must be."

Then and there I chided him for the years of teaching he had heard but failed to take into his life. (I was well aware of the Bible studies and fellowship groups to which he had been exposed.) After reviewing passages of Scripture setting forth the Spirit's very personal work as Teacher and Sanctifier, I asked Jake to kneel at his chair and confess his sin of careless neglect of truth that was very available to him. I warned him of the jeopardy of those who "deliberately forget" precious teachings (2 Peter 3:5); it is better not to know the truth than to know it and then ignore it (2:21). He did confess his neglect of truth and then welcomed the Holy Spirit to fill and command his life.

Days later, my wife and I were guests in their home for fellowship and coffee. Their children were not present, so Elizabeth took the opportunity to update us on their improved relationship. "I scarcely know the man sitting there," she said, gesturing toward her husband. "He is so changed!" What a delight to hear her describe the changes—it was nothing other than a catalog of the Spirit's new fruit in Jake's character. The usually fiery fellow sat with head slightly and humbly bowed, radiating a quiet smile. Here were visible footprints of the invisible Holy Spirit!

## Simply Knowing Is Not All There Is to It

Understanding how Jesus represents us before God in his life, death, resurrection, and ascension must be followed by personal faith. Comprehension requires appropriation. In other words, we must *take* what we *know*. A central work of the Holy Spirit is to help us take into our personal experience all that Jesus is and does for us.

Remember, God's purpose in laying the penalty for our sins on the shoulders of the Substitute, his Son and our Savior, is to release us from death so that we might live for him (2 Cor. 5:15). Only the Holy Spirit can bring that purpose of the crucifixion to its fruition in our lives. A study of Romans 8 will show God's determination to get his children out of their natural, selfish, sinful living, and just as clearly we see that the Holy Spirit's presence is dominant in these verses. Furthermore, according to verse 13, he is the assisting means by which we put to death the urge to sin: "If by the Spirit you put to death the misdeeds of the body, you will live."

This verse presses me to follow through with what I know of the work of Christ *in my place* and move to claim in faith Christ *in my life*. The former frees us from our impossible, overwhelming debt of sin, and we are for the first time in our lives free to call on God as our Father. This new freedom must then be used in earnest prayer for the Spirit's assistance to put down our own sinful urges and to live for our Lord and Savior Jesus Christ.

It should be clear, then, that Jesus settles the legal charges against us by what he does *instead of* us, but the stranglehold of evil attitudes, desires, and actions must be broken by what he will do *in* us by the Spirit. As we concur with the Spirit, his powerful hand leads and empowers us. See Romans 8:14 and Galatians 5:25. The Holy Spirit makes Christ clear to our understanding and real in our living. He inaugurates a deep, life-changing association between himself and the spirit of each child of God.

Look into the nature of this life in the Spirit, and you will see clearly that it requires that both our understanding and our will must be active. God does not simply do things *for* us and *to* us, but he works *within* us as we understand truth and concur with it all. How sad it is, then, when preachers and teachers turn their hearers' minds off their moral obligations (in response to truth) and turn them instead to grandiose, happy promises of physical and material prosperity that will supposedly end all trial and suffering. Surely, that delusion is utterly foreign to the apostle Paul's testimony in 2 Corinthians. See 1:8, for example, with the very next verse explaining the benefits from this discipline. Paul's harassment, conflicts, and fears are frankly stated in 7:5, but see how all is made into a delicious sandwich of providence with the verses that precede and follow, which employ the words "my joy knows no bounds" and "my joy was greater than ever." So he concludes, "That is why, for Christ's sake, I delight in weaknesses, in insults, in hardships, in persecutions, in difficulties. For when I am weak, then I am strong" (12:10).

Job and 1 Peter are two books devoted entirely to the challenging subject of the believer in trial. The joy promised as a fruit of the Spirit does not rule out the need for patient endurance, which is also provided by the Spirit.

## God's Spirit Takes on the World

Not only does the Spirit minister in the hearts and lives of God's children, but he also conducts a ministry to the world of sinful men and women, making effective the testimony of believers. "When the Counselor comes, whom I will send to you from the Father . . . he will testify about me. And you also must testify"

(John 15:26-27).

Again, it is imperative that we see the essential connection between the resurrection and ascension of Christ and the moving of the Holy Spirit on the lost people of this age. Even among believers, however, too little evidence appears in what we now "see and hear" (see Acts 2:32-33) that our Lord has indeed sent the Spirit from his position there at God's right hand to do his work here. Before his ascension, Jesus promised,

> But I tell you the truth: It is for your good that I am going away. Unless I go away, the Counselor will not come to you; but if I go, I will send him to you. When he comes, he will convict the world of guilt in regard to sin and righteousness and judgment: in regard to sin, because men do not believe in me; in regard to righteousness, because I am going to the Father, where you can see me no longer; and in regard to judgment, because the prince of this world now stands condemned. (John 16:7-11)

In this crucial passage Jesus states the threefold ministry of the Spirit in the hearts and minds of our sinful world. The Spirit's task is to bow worldlings under a sense of guilt regarding their sin, their lack of righteousness, and the imminence of judgment. Then Jesus goes on to make clear why the Spirit's moving is absolutely indispensable if this threefold ministry is to be accomplished. Look carefully at these three questions and at Jesus' explanations.

*Why is the Spirit so needed to convince sinners regarding their sin?* The answer is put simply by our Lord: "Because men do not believe in me" (v. 9). How can a world that stresses tolerance and indiscrimination toward almost everything except those things that have reference to Jesus Christ ever come to true faith in him? Sated in immorality, pleasure, and materialism, the world enjoys the pleasures of sin for their brief season and simply will not recognize and repent of its sin—until the Spirit of God pays a personal, individual visit. Believers who attempt to win their friends for Christ have exactly three alternatives: (1) speak to them in the power of the Spirit, (2) speak to them with human strength and find them to be as resistant as granite blocks, or (3) speak easy words, allowing them to skirt true conviction of their guilt and perhaps "accept Jesus" without forsaking the very sin that the Spirit is sent to convince them of.

*Why is the Spirit so needed to convince sinners regarding righteousness?* "Because," explains Jesus, "I am going to the Father, where you can see me no longer" (v. 10). Jesus the Righteous One brought light into the world and exposed unrighteousness. Now it is the Holy Spirit who must convince our age of righteousness, which is so foreign to a society that has loosened its moral moorings and is adrift with no idea of absolutes. For its remedy, this moral confusion pervading culture today needs the very ministry that Jesus assigns to the Holy Spirit in John 16.

Far beyond convincing society of moral right and wrong, the Spirit's great work is seen when "in the gospel a righteousness from God is revealed" (Rom. 1:17). This same epistle declares that "now a righteousness from God, apart from law, has been made known. . . . This righteousness from God comes through faith in Jesus Christ to all who believe" (3:21-22).

*Why is the Spirit so needed to convince sinners regarding judgment?* "Because the prince of this world now stands condemned," says Jesus. See our world chained to Satan's will, marching in lockstep with his rhythms and believing the same lie that Adam and Eve believed, "You will not surely die" (Gen. 3:4). Measure the proportions of this eternally fatal error—that of obeying a prince whose own condemnation and overthrow were pronounced 2,000 years ago by the Lord Jesus Christ as he faced the cross: "Now is the time for judgment on this world; now the prince of this world will be driven out" (John 12:31).

Our world's blindness is fatal, and only the Holy Spirit can remedy the tragedy of sworn allegiance to a doomed spiritual ruler. How aware and alarmed are believers? How many are pleading with our Lord to restore the quickening power of the Holy Spirit among us? God has warned, "These things you have done and I kept silent; you thought I was altogether like you. But I will rebuke you and accuse you to your face" (Ps. 50:21).

May the Spirit arrest men and women from the grave peril of looking forward to heaven while heading to hell.

## 2. Christ There for Us, Making Intercession

Our Savior's triumphant welcome into heaven and his session at the Father's right hand must have major impact on our lives. The glorious reception given Jesus shows the Father's full acceptance of our Lord's payment for our sins. We must not tarnish Christ's honor by standing back in earth's shadows, failing to enter heaven's courts by faith.

The apostle Paul reminds us forcefully that when we stood as God's enemies, we were yet so loved that God reconciled us by giving his Son to die for us. Then follows the exclamation, "How much more . . . shall we be saved through his life!" (Rom 5:10). Hebrews 7:25 adds, "He always lives to intercede for them."

Faulty ideas of Christ's intercession weaken faith. We often feel far removed from heaven's gate and, as a result, feel as if we must beg our way up a prayer chain-of-command. Jesus sets aside this flawed notion in John 16:26: "In that day you will ask in my name. I am not saying that I will ask the Father on your behalf." In the next verse he adds these heartwarming words: "No, the Father himself loves you because you have loved me and have believed that I came from God." Instead of feeling like beggars, we ought to act like the young son of a company president who bounds through his dad's big office door with an innocent liberty—to the envy of corporate officials. I will have much more to say about this precious subject when we come to the study of prayer in chapter 8.

The intercession of our Lord is not merely an appendage to Calvary's propitiation. Rather, it is a blessed assurance that we are welcome in glory. Our Advocate is well positioned with the Judge! God's children are assured of a favorable outcome to their cause.

> He who did not spare his own Son, but gave him up for us all—how will he not also, along with him, graciously give us all things? Who will bring any charge against those whom God has chosen? It is God who justifies. Who is he that condemns? Christ Jesus, who died—more than that, who was raised to life—is at the right hand of God and is also interceding for us. Who shall separate us from the love of Christ? (Rom. 8:32-35)

In deep humiliation, Jesus made atonement for us on the cross. In great glory, Jesus intercedes for us and applies benefits to us that he has won at so great a price.

> For this reason he had to be made like his brothers in every way, in order that he might become a merciful and faithful high priest in service to God, and that he might make atonement for the sins of the people. Because he himself suffered when he was tempted, he is able to help those who are being tempted. (Heb. 2:17-18)

> Therefore, since we have a great high priest who has gone through the heavens, Jesus the Son of God, let us hold

firmly to the faith we profess. For we do not have a high priest who is unable to sympathize with our weaknesses, but we have one who has been tempted in every way, just as we are—yet was without sin. Let us then approach the throne of grace with confidence, so that we may receive mercy and find grace to help us in our time of need. (Heb. 4:14-16)

## 3. We Here for Christ—His Ambassadors

Our life with Jesus does not consign us to a dogmatic reliance on a dry, flat belief-system. The glorious Christ now resides within each believer through the living presence of the Holy Spirit. Not only is Christ in us, but we are in him, our Representative and Head. We are *there* with him, and he is *here* with us.

The privileges and authority belonging to Christ's family members are experienced only to the extent that we understand his exaltation. Once crowned with thorns, the symbol of the curse of sin (Gen. 3:17-19), our Savior bore the curse itself in his death, and now he is crowned with a splendor beyond anything that Adam and Eve ever knew before their fall.

I appeal to you, my reader, to look long at our Lord, "who has gone into heaven and is at God's right hand—with angels, authorities and powers in submission to him" (1 Peter 3:22). Is your relationship with such a Lord fully evidenced in your life? Christ's power and glory in heaven is commended to us for our continual meditation so that earth's perspectives will be reshaped by that exalted view. "Since, then, you have been raised with Christ, set your hearts on things above, where Christ is seated at the right hand of God. Set your minds on things above, not on earthly things" (Col. 3:1-2).

"We are therefore Christ's ambassadors, as though God were

making his appeal through us. We implore you on Christ's behalf: Be reconciled to God" (2 Cor. 5:20). We speak on the behalf of—in the name of—the One who is Lord of all. All our witness must be made to men and women in the Lord's authority, and all our prayers must be made to God in the name of the Lord Jesus. (I shall have much more to say about these ministries in part 2.)

Heaven is much too closed to us today. As a result, we are weak in our ambassadorship for Christ. That commission seems far beyond us unless we see that heavenly blessings are available right now (Eph. 1:3). Our royal position with Christ is to be grasped right now (Eph. 2:6). In his name we may stand "strong in the Lord and in his mighty power" (Eph. 6:10).

By faith's eye, we may go "aloft," as needed. Faithful Stephen looked above and beyond the angry lynchers raging against him, and he was buoyed up by what he saw: "I see heaven open and the Son of Man standing at the right hand of God" (Acts 7:56).

The Lord Jesus Christ ran his race on earth with a focused view of "the joy set before him," a goal that enabled him to endure the cross and totally discount its shame (Heb. 12:2). For him, the glory awaiting completely overshadowed the prospect of death, so he prays in John 17, "And now, Father, glorify me in your presence with the glory I had with you before the world began" (v. 5), and "Father, I want those you have given me to be with me where I am, and to see my glory, the glory you have given me because you loved me before the creation of the world" (v. 24).

With this perspective now in mind, consider what Hebrews 12:2 orders us to do: *Let us fix our eyes on him*—on the One who looked to joy ahead and above. As you run your race (that is, live your life), make him your joy beyond and above. Believers are so bonded with our Lord Jesus that his present elevation in the heavenlies should have rich results in our life here on earth.

## 4. We Together with Him Forever—Our Hope

Hope heals human brokenness. The prospect of Christ coming again, literally and visibly, is intended to bring a kind of spiritual vitality that enriches and heals. Because hope is so important a subject, I have included a separate study on it in appendix 4, where the emphasis is on hope's strength and how it works. Here, we will continue our concentration on the person of "Christ Jesus our hope," as 1 Timothy 1:1 puts it.

In addition to his occupation in heaven dealing with our immediate needs, our Lord Jesus is preparing our eternal home and providing for our rest, there with him (John 14:1-4). He will overcome death totally. No more cowering before that enemy. No more burden of having to include death in our planning. Dying is like moving. At first we are so happy with the house and property where we live. We declare that we will never move. But as time passes, the windows and doors loosen, and cold drafts are felt. The roof leaks. In spite of our efforts, weeds invade the prized lawn and flower gardens, and the cellar floods as cracks in the walls and foundation increase beyond what patching can fix. Gathering clutter makes the once-spacious rooms shrivel in size. The very foundations seem shaky. More and more we feel that leaving here will be a relief!

Shattered dreams or failing health might benefit us if they press us into the arms of Jesus and encourage us to heed Peter's admonition to "set your hope fully on the grace to be given you when Jesus Christ is revealed" (1 Peter 1:13). In the important meantime, we who "hope in Christ" may "be for the praise of his glory" as we are "marked in him with a seal, the promised Holy Spirit, who is a deposit guaranteeing our inheritance" (Eph. 1:12-14). Countless other Scriptures also tie earth to heaven, us to Christ, and the present to the future.

(For discussion of the larger question of why forgiven people still die, see appendix 5.)

## One Dimension of Hope

The ultimate object of our hope, then, is our Lord himself, and this hope is two-dimensional. Our life perspectives and way of living are to be shaped by the two dimensions of this hope. One dimension involves Jesus Christ's future return in power and great glory, when he visibly visits our realm, consummates history, and establishes the eternal state. Titus 2:11-14 makes it clear that God's grace aims at teaching and training us in godliness "while we wait for the blessed hope—the glorious appearing of our great God and Savior, Jesus Christ."

Tears streamed down Paul's face as he saw this very hope trifled with by some in the congregation at Philippi. Their appetites and desires riveted their minds to earthly things and turned them into adversaries of Christ (Phil. 3:18). Verse 20 shows what this hope holds on to: "But our citizenship is in heaven. And we eagerly await a Savior from there, the Lord Jesus Christ, who, by the power that enables him to bring everything under his control, will transform our lowly bodies so that they will be like his glorious body."

## Another Dimension of Hope

How can it be that such a momentous prospect as the incarnate Creator visibly invading the world fails to figure into today's affairs—even for many Christians? Consider this explanation: Those who overlook the magnitude of Christ's *present* glory and occupation likely have little genuine concern for any *future* involvement with him. That is, many are not looking for him in the future because they are overlooking him now. Their interest in eschatology is more academic than spiritual. The living Jesus has withdrawn.

The second dimension of hope concerns our Lord's present engagement in the heavenlies. As we revisit this topic, it will become apparent that both dimensions—the future happenings (the second coming) and the very present activities of Jesus Christ—are virtually inseparable. Carelessness toward either area of truth means the total loss of vital hope, and we are left cherishing worn labels of truth—truth that once was, or perhaps never really was, ours.

Keep it clearly in mind that Christ's present splendor has not replaced his incarnate human nature, but it does make his union with us more remarkable. Study reverently, prayerfully Colossians 2:9-10: "For in Christ all the fullness of the Deity lives in bodily form, and you have been given fullness in Christ, who is the head over every power and authority."

Remember also what we covered earlier in this chapter regarding our position of identity with Christ our Representative. His place and accomplishments in the heavenlies are on our behalf, and we must claim all these benefits just as we believed and received his position and work on our behalf on earth.

## Until

In both the Old and New Testaments the little word "until" is employed to link the two dimensions of our hope in Christ—that of his present and his future activities. See what the prophetic Psalm 110 reveals to us in its first verse: "The LORD [God our Father] says to my Lord [the Messiah]: 'Sit at my right hand until I make your enemies a footstool for your feet.'" Then 1 Corinthians 15:25 uses "until" in the same way. As we return to this crucial chapter, however, we will focus our investigation on the larger context of verse 25, including verses 20-28.

²⁰But Christ has indeed been raised from the dead, the firstfruits of those who have fallen asleep. ²¹For since death came through a man, the resurrection of the dead comes also through a man. ²²For as in Adam all die, so in Christ all will be made alive. ²³But each in his own turn: Christ, the firstfruits; then, when he comes, those who belong to him. ²⁴Then the end will come, when he hands over the kingdom to God the Father after he has destroyed all dominion, authority and power. ²⁵For he must reign until he has put all his enemies under his feet. ²⁶The last enemy to be destroyed is death. ²⁷For he "has put everything under his feet." Now when it says that "everything" has been put under him, it is clear that this does not include God himself, who put everything under Christ. ²⁸When he has done this, then the Son himself will be made subject to him who put everything under him, so that God may be all in all.

In highlighting salient points from the above text, I have in mind two objectives: (1) to show that Christ's present activities are directly related to the future, and (2) to expose the enormity of the sin of treating lightly what Jesus is *now* about (regardless of how much special interest we might take in matters of prophecy). With this text before you, notice these truths, taken in order of the verses.

1. Adam and Christ are like contrasting fountains. The stream from the former brings death, whereas the latter yields resurrection life (vv. 20-22).
2. The resurrected Savior lives as guarantee of our resurrection to follow (v. 23).
3. His return and our resurrection are joined (v. 23).
4. The end (that is, the final, eternal state) awaits a momentous transfer, or handing over, of the kingdom to God our Father (v. 24).

5. The *present* shines with the Messiah's honor, as God continues the universal enterprise of subduing all evil under the feet of Jesus Christ (v. 25).

6. This process of putting all things under Christ's control will end only when death is forever destroyed (v. 26).

Before dealing with the seventh and final truth, pause with me for a further look at the present state. Christ the Lord is said to be seated and waiting, but also to be reigning and warring. Psalm 110 pictures him not only receiving the seat and designation of honor but also crushing opposition and hastening onward like an invincible warrior in pursuit of final victory. All this activity is said to be taking place as the Father grants victory to the Son he honors. In turn, it is essential for Christ's followers to understand that the flag of battle has been passed on to us and that we are to conquer in Christ's name, claiming and insisting by faith that our great foe is defeated, even the one who so long has held the power of death. The victory for which we fight is certainly ours. Christ wins for us all that the Father gives to him. His present intercession and ministries in the heavenlies guarantee that what is his may be ours. (In part 2 we shall investigate further how we are to share actively in this great warfare.)

For now, let us be encouraged with the significance of the word "until" (v. 25). All the present stress is only *until* things now transpiring lead into future glory and things everlasting.

The final salient truth set forth in the Scripture section under discussion is given prominence as the ultimate divine objective.

7. By putting together verses 24 and 28, the picture is brought into focus: "Then the end will come, when he hands over the kingdom to God the Father. . . . When he has done this, then the Son himself will be made subject to him who put everything under him, so that God may be all in all."

Remember from our earlier discussions that there is no essential, eternal subordination between the three persons of the Trinity. The Son, however, has voluntarily taken a human nature also, and on earth he humbled himself in servanthood and suffering as a sacrifice for our sin. By resurrection he was released from the frailties of the flesh, but he has not ceased to be a member of the human race—our Head and Lord. God is even now working in all events of history "to bring all things in heaven and on earth together under one head, even Christ" (Eph. 1:10).

Then, when every knee is brought to bow in submission to our glorious Head, none will doubt that he is "the ruler of the kings of the earth," "the ruler of God's creation," and "King of Kings and Lord of Lords" (Rev. 1:5; 3:14; 19:16). At that moment will transpire the most momentous movement in God's rule of the universe. Our Lord Jesus Christ, Head and Savior of the human family, will lead all into a position of submission to the everlasting Father. Never, ever again in the entire universe will there be even the slightest hint of rebellion or whim of evil or twinge of pain or tear of grief. Peace and righteousness forever!

# MY TESTIMONY

The truths we are discussing in this book did not present themselves to me in clear light all at once—not by any means! Rather, I spent five, ten, or perhaps as many as fifteen years of my life laboring to grasp some of it. Frequently, I would take stock of my life, inventorying the fruit. And there was some, but I knew there was more to be had from God. "Is this all there is to it, for me, on this side of Pentecost?!" I would ask aloud as I begged God for more. My primary burden was not in the area of accomplishments for Christ. I was more concerned with attitudes and actions that were not under control of the Holy Spirit. The Christlike life that was promised and commanded in Scripture seemed to elude me.

On one occasion, in my early manhood, when a longed-for core principle finally became understandable to me, I was so happy that immediately, that very evening, I invited seven or eight couples to our home so that I might share with them my new treasures, for which I had so long sought. Even on such short notice, all the invited couples came and were obviously impacted by the truths shared. We ended our evening by kneeling in prayer and committing ourselves, with a new and deeper meaning, to our God and Savior.

That meeting in our home was an important turning point in my spiritual life and ministry. Now I could see decidedly that truths revealed by God were teachings he wanted understood and appropriated. Furthermore, the task of the teacher was to make the insights available with the Spirit's help so that others who truly hungered for truth might be spared futile years of striving.

In reviewing my own pilgrimage, I have often asked the question, What took me so long? Was I not longing to know Jesus Christ, and was I not pressing to know truth that would set me free? And did I not seek out teachers and listen carefully as they expounded the very texts that promised the liberty I sought? As I responded to their challenges, was I not sincere? What hindered me? I am not sure I know the complete answer to this last question, but I pray that I may shorten the path for some who read what I here share from my own experience.

As a very small boy, I longed for and prayed for salvation. Gradually, I understood that Jesus' suffering and death had reference to my sins, and I came to a confident rest in God's forgiveness. In my later boyhood, however, I saw that what Jesus did in my behalf was one thing, but what he wanted to do in my life was another matter. I understood that he died for my sins, but this insight only made my ongoing struggle against continuing failures more painful.

Years of personal searching followed. At times it was very intense. My reading, praying, conversing, and listening to "deeper life" messages intensified the inquiry but did not meet my need. I was, by now, already in pastoral ministry. I even preached on the texts that promised full release and personal liberty in Jesus Christ. I could talk to others about the truth, but I could not "see" it for myself. Romans 6–8 drew me like a magnet. I knew my answers were surely there, but I could not get hold of it all.

I painfully searched for each answer in a separated, disjointed sense, not realizing that there might be a key concept that was missing. Around and around I went, being told on the one hand that I was crucified with Christ, but on the other seeing that I was very alive to temptations and sin. Finally, I went back to the fifth chapter of Romans and got my footing and bearings corrected. Flashes of new insight, one after the other, began to reveal Jesus to me in fresh ways. I saw more clearly how he stood in my place in the fallen family of Adam. My guilt was credited to him as he died on the cross. He was my Representative. It took a while, but the gradual dawning brought this steady light: the flip side of having Jesus take my punishment was that God then counted me as having been executed when my Representative died.

This insight opened my eyes to let the Scripture mean what it said when it told me that I died with Jesus. I treasured this revelation. I put it in my knapsack and quickened my pilgrim step. But again, discouragements returned, in spite of my newly stored insights. I could not seem to follow directions and put down sinful desires and walk in the Spirit.

Teachings on the resurrection of Jesus, so often joined to statements about his crucifixion, began to draw me to search into the connection between our Lord's dying for me and his rising for me. I saw that his death was a completed act and, in a sense, contrasted with his resurrection. For example, Romans 6:10 states, "The death he died, he died to sin once for all; but the life he lives, he lives to God."

This section of Scripture was a powerful help to me, freeing me from errant teachings regarding the meaning of my "dying to sin." I saw that verse 10 plainly said that Jesus died to sin. The only possible way to understand this idea is to say that our Savior died with respect to the legal condemnation that was mine. God appointed Jesus as my representative, so when he died as my substitute, God counts it that I died to the guilt that was mine.

I read in verse 11 that "in the same way" I was to count

myself "dead to sin." That settled it! I did not have to imagine myself numb and insensitive to the pull of sin. Rather, I was to look at the cross and embrace that death as my full payment for sin. This truth, then, freed me both from damnation and from the guilty conscience, and it enabled me to take what was next for me. And there it is, in the adjoining phrase of verse 11: "alive to God in Christ Jesus." I am here directed to step into the benefits of both the cross and the resurrection. I am to claim by faith that both these saving works of Christ are assigned to me by the gracious Father in heaven.

Now I saw that Christ's death settles my legal debt (I died with and through him) and that Christ's resurrection brings new life to me (I rose with him). The former alters my record in heaven, or my standing before God. But the resurrection brings new life to me. No need for me to flounder about, I realized, because the Spirit that raised Jesus from the dead has moved into my life and truly conveys to me Christ's new life. See Romans 8:11.

The treasured phrase "in Christ" reminds us believers that we are united with Christ. Our union is an official one and refers to our legal identity with Jesus. Furthermore, our union with Christ is also an organic one, in that the Holy Spirit imparts in our experience the benefits Christ has for us. Believers "live in him, and he in them" (1 John 3:24).

My deserved execution for sin was carried out in such a way (by proxy) that I am spared to present myself to God as an instrument for expressing his life on earth, in the sphere where I live. See Romans 6:13 and Galatians 2:20. Transformations in outlook and in ministry are bound to follow in the heart and life that yield to the truths we are discussing. For me, as the insights came, every part of ministry was changed. The exalted Head was freer to build his church according to what Scripture said, rather than by what human tradition dictated. The alterations, as I grew into them, have influenced the subject matter of the final half of this writing and give hope, in spite of our confusions and failures.

# PART 2

# CRUCIAL PRACTICES NOW WEAKENED

# 7

# FAITH, THE WAY THAT
# PLEASES GOD

The study of faith gathers in its embrace both major parts of *Bringing Christ Back*. Great truths discussed in part 1 are perceived by faith, and then they must be practiced by faith, as taught in this second part. Particularly the next chapter, on prayer, is related to faith.

Scripture makes clear the relationship between faith and the other subjects covered in this book. First, faith comes from gospel truths ("Faith comes from hearing the message, and the message is heard through the word of Christ," Rom. 10:17), and faith also is needed to grasp these truths ("The message they heard was of no value to them, because those who heard did not combine it with faith," Heb. 4:2). Second, faith is crucial for prayer ("If you believe [that is, have faith], you will receive whatever you ask for in prayer," Matt. 21:22).

Faith is exercised through prayer. Apart from humble, earnest prayer, faith either fades or turns to presumption. It is dangerous to walk far without much prayer.

Faith is trusting God. This relationship is sustained through prayerfully embracing more and more truth; that is, faith is exercised by interacting with God through prayer. We on the one hand view and accept by faith all that Christ is before his Father; on the other hand, through faith and prayer we exercise our resulting responsibilities to extend his rule and share in the subjugation of evil and in the establishment of his righteous ways today.

Faith is a subject prominent throughout Scripture. It is defined, explained, illustrated, and theologically expounded. Sadly, what God places before us with such emphasis, we too often let sink beneath the horizon of practical usefulness.

Faith is the way to get on with God, and indeed "without faith it is impossible to please God" (Heb. 11:6). Faith is the instrument for gaining blessings and resisting evil. The writer of Hebrews invests an entire chapter (11) in expounding the powerful workings of faith. Paul wrote extensively about the very anatomy of faith, citing the elderly Abraham's example: "Yet he did not waver through unbelief regarding the promise of God, but was strengthened in his faith and gave glory to God, being fully persuaded that God had power to do what he had promised" (Rom. 4:20-21).

In the light of this text, we see that faith is the way God's needy child can connect with the life and power of the Almighty. God is specially honored when he is trusted. As the child of God grows in faith, he or she develops a restful reliance on God himself and on what he says. Thus, as we believe, all the rich benefits of what we have covered thus far in this book are channeled to us. And thus we are spared attempting to live the Christian life without the impartation of divine strength. Nothing is as grueling as attempting to live the Christian life with a broken faith-connection.

God has promised to supply all that we need, "so that in all things at all times, having all that you need, you will abound in every good work" (2 Cor. 9:8). "Need," though, must be defined as whatever we require to fulfill God's will and purposes in us and through us. We might not want what we need, but faith looks beyond any uncertainty and enables us to see more perfectly God's ways. Faith opens the essential channel from God's supplies to our areas of need—whether that be a need of fortitude or one of understanding, love, patience (or any other fruit of the Spirit), material and physical sustenance, ability to serve, or anything else.

The opening verse of Hebrews 11 illuminates faith by showing how it gives us gracious verification in two dimensions that otherwise would be beyond our reach: (1) our future hopes and (2) things unseen, invisible: "Now faith is being sure of what we hope for and certain of what we do not see."

God is here said to give both an assurance to the believing one regarding what is ahead and also a certainty about God himself. In verse 6 faith is said to please God by grasping the realness of God's existence and by perceiving that he will surely reward the one who earnestly seeks him. See again the two categories in this verse also: the invisible and the future. These two dimensions of faith are seen in the lives of the faithful ones we meet in this chapter. For example, Moses remained true to God "because he was looking ahead to his reward," and "he persevered because he saw him who is invisible" (vv. 26-27). Job also maintained faith-contact with the Invisible One and sustained assurance concerning the future; therefore he testified, "But he knows the way that I take; when he has tested me, I will come forth as gold" (Job 23:10).

## Grasping the Past, Present, and Future by Faith

All our interaction with Jesus' person and work in the past, the present, and the future is done by means of faith. At the outset of our spiritual life we came to trust in our Lord himself and his death as the propitiation for our sins. By faith, we claimed what Scripture revealed to us, just as the apostle Paul tells us in Romans 1:17: "For in the gospel a righteousness from God is revealed, a righteousness that is by faith from first to last, just as it is written: 'The righteous will live by faith.'"

The final six words of this verse form a familiar biblical maxim to keep us ever aware that our entire Christian life is "by faith." That is, our spiritual lot is cast in that mode, and by the means of faith we continue to draw divine strength to live a new life.

"By grace you have been saved, through faith—and this not from yourselves, it is the gift of God" (Eph. 2:8). Paul goes on to show how, from the very outset of the Christian life, this living by faith strips away pride. Looking at the cross, I am led to repentance, not only because of the shame caused by my sins, but also because of my utter inability to contribute anything toward my salvation. I am shut up to faith alone, a complete reliance on the blood of Christ to atone for my sins and the righteousness of Christ to clothe me as I stand before God. "So then, just as you received Christ Jesus as Lord, continue to live in him" (Col. 2:6). Therefore, "We fix our eyes not on what is seen, but on what is unseen"; and again, "We live by faith, not by sight" (2 Cor. 4:18 and 5:7).

At the end of chapter 3 above, I discussed the two dimensions of grace—what Christ does *in our place* and what he does *in our lives*. Quite obviously, faith must take hold of each of these manifestations of God's goodness in differing manners. Untold misery comes to those who attempt to add their own merit to what Christ has done for our right standing before God. Untold misery is likewise caused when Christians attempt to believe hard enough that somehow our Lord works out their sanctification in their stead, without concurrence on their part. We believe in order to be saved, and then because we are saved, we obey, through the help of the Spirit of God.

As the Spirit engenders and sustains hope within believing hearts, he guarantees future glorification, even to those who are engulfed in suffering. Faith relates easily to God's Spirit. This partnership is strong enough to face down death with a shout of victory.

> Now it is God who has made us for this very purpose and has given us the Spirit as a deposit, guaranteeing what is to come. Therefore we are always confident and know that as long as we are at home in the body we are away from the Lord. We live by faith, not by sight. We are confident, I say, and would prefer to be away from the body and at home with the Lord. So we make it our goal to please him, whether we are at home in the body or away from it. (2 Cor. 5:5-9)

These powerful words are filled with nutrients for faith, enabling us who are "at home in the body" to live with unshakable confidence, even as death threatens. What the world regards as sunset, children of faith see as eternal life's sunrise.

## Concluding Thoughts

- More than the existence and activities of God are embraced by faith. As we grow in faith under the tutelage of the Spirit, using the Word, we are brought into closeness with God. No longer are we held hostage by our own limited resources. The Lord Jesus Christ stands by us with all his assets.
- If the life we currently are living does not demand real faith, we are not following Christ as we ought.

- Beware of thinking that living by faith is in itself a test or trial. Far from that, faith is the way *through* a trial. Faith is the hand that touches God and takes from him his provisions of blessing. God's privileged children of faith can rise on wings of faith, aided by the wind of the Spirit, while earth-bound souls only move up and down runways, dodging traffic.

- Straining to believe hard enough can never make what is not so become so. God does not break the laws he makes, and we cannot try to use faith to break the law of contradiction. For example, I cannot be living in ongoing sinful defeat and yet believe that I am victorious in Christ. If I deliberately toy with sin, it is impossible to connect with God and receive grace "to keep me covered."

- Finally, we must not take for granted the faith that operates in our hearts as if it were a low-maintenance item. God sees it otherwise:

> Now for a little while you may have had to suffer grief in all kinds of trials. These have come so that your faith—of greater worth than gold, which perishes even though refined by fire—may be proved genuine and may result in praise, glory and honor when Jesus Christ is revealed. Though you have not seen him, you love him; and even though you do not see him now, you believe in him and are filled with an inexpressible and glorious joy, for you are receiving the goal of your faith, the salvation of your souls. (1 Peter 1:6-9)

# 8

# RULING WITH CHRIST
# THROUGH PRAYER

Perhaps because of tending my wife, an Alzheimer's patient, since the early 1990s, I have found that prayer has become less a subject for writing and discussion and more a total way of life. God's disciplines aim at pressing into our lives what is contrary to our human nature.

As we begin this crucial area of study, consider its connection with what we have already covered. Nothing is so powerful as the right kind of praying. Nothing is so pitiful as wrong praying. When Christ is in his place of glory and authority before the mind's eye of the believer, mountains move. Conversely, if our Lord and his work are not clearly in mind as the petitions are uttered, little will come of our efforts. Many human explanations have been devised to excuse and defend the lack of specific answers to prayer.

The withdrawal of our Lord's presence is both a result and a cause of defective prayer. He might be distanced from us and our prayers rendered ineffective by any one of three reasons.

First, we have not taken hold of the core truths about Christ. If Christ's person, work, and present position are not plain to our mind and heart as intercessors, little will come of our praying.

111

Here is a remedy: Take the time to review prayerfully the material in part 1, responding as God's Spirit might direct you. Then, as you pray, continually renew your grip on the truths you have learned.

Second, we have tolerated sinful practices and attitudes. Since "the prayer of a righteous man is powerful and effective" (James 5:16), what must we conclude if our prayers are not powerful and effective? It is virtually impossible for a boy who is grieving his father to have confident expectation that his requests will be granted. Scripture teaches that one who is unstable and doubting "should not think he will receive anything from the Lord" (James 1:7). James goes on to state that selfish, sinful motives in prayer will most certainly prevent our receiving answers (4:1-3). Other Scriptures such as the following must also be reckoned with:

> If anyone turns a deaf ear to the law, even his prayers are detestable. (Prov. 28:9)

> When you spread out your hands in prayer, I will hide my eyes from you; even if you offer many prayers, I will not listen. Your hands are full of blood. (Isa. 1:15)

> You have covered yourself with a cloud so that no prayer can get through. (Lam. 3:44)

Third, we have failed to grow in our experience of prayer. Lessons learned in prayer must be assimilated continuously as we deepen in our walk with Christ. These lessons are indispensable for spiritual growth, for praying is associated with growth.

### The Profound Alignment of Prayer

Most people who pray sincerely will be like one of two young brothers I picture caught in a cold and violent rainstorm.

Leaning into the gale, they struggle forward, lifting their heads only briefly to keep on their pathway. Finally, an upward glance lifts the hearts of the frightened lads. Immediately before them stands a large, well-lit home. The older boy quickens his pace and runs ahead to seek an entrance for them. Calling back to his younger brother to follow, he is welcomed within. But the little one hesitates to enter and stays outside in the cold rain, gaining what solace he can from thoughts of his older brother's place in the warmth and blessing of the mansion.

Our life of prayer must not be conducted at such a distance and in such a manner. Distressing storms will surely overtake us. How sad to stand outside, reading Scripture and attempting to capture in our minds the significance of Jesus' entry into the heavenlies to open the way for us! Perhaps we try to strengthen this musing by delighting in what will one day be ours when Jesus returns for us. What we most need, though, is to enter *now* where Jesus is and "draw near to God" (Heb. 10:22).

Standing ready to accompany us as we enter the presence of God is the Holy Spirit. Be assured that the gracious Spirit assists only those who, with understanding, see Jesus Christ in his place at the Father's right hand. Scripture says of our Savior, "In him and through faith in him we may approach God with freedom and confidence" (Eph. 3:12). In addition, "Through him we both [Jew and Gentile] have access to the Father by one Spirit" (2:18).

Here, then, is the complete alignment. In prayer we are to make our approach to the Father through the Son and by means of the Spirit's guidance. With such an alignment available, our prayers should consistently be fruitful and effective. Despite this profound arrangement, however, some Christians find prayer burdensome, even distasteful. Their praying is rather like an automobile out of alignment: it drives hard.

Undoubtedly, the most significant section of Scripture on this matter of proper alignment in prayer is three chapters in John's gospel (14–16), followed by our Lord's own chapter-long prayer (17). See the great importance Jesus gives to our praying. Jesus' followers are to do "even greater things" (14:12) than his own, he says, "because I am going to the Father. And I will do whatever you ask in my name, so that the Son may bring glory to the Father. You may ask me for anything in my name, and I will do it" (vv. 12-14). Our works are simply what he is doing through us as we pray. Or putting it another way, his works are now done through his praying people. The disciples' "greater things" (v. 12) are the same accomplishments that "I [Jesus] will do" (vv. 13, 14) as we pray. Pride is limited as we realize that the Lord is doing his work through us—as we pray. What we see as answers to our prayers is really the Son bringing glory to the Father (v. 13), the Vine bringing honor to the Gardner by producing abundant fruit through the branches (15:8). We too are honored, however, in that we are privileged to rule with Christ through prayer. Kingdom affairs are administered through our prayers.

In both verses 13 and 14 of chapter 14, we are taught to ask in Christ's name. In the latter verse he adds, "Ask me." The Lord Jesus Christ invites us, "Ask me . . . in my name." He is our Lord, and he is our Mediator. Thus he says to us: *Ask me* as your Lord; *ask in my name*—through me—as your Mediator.

In the light of these words, what are we to make of the following instruction from Jesus, two chapters later? "In that day you will no longer ask me anything. I tell you the truth, my Father will give you whatever you ask in my name. Until now you have not asked for anything in my name. Ask and you will receive, and your joy will be complete" (John 16:23-24). At first glance it might seem that Jesus is contradicting himself, saying both "Don't ask me" and "Ask me." Not so. He is simply preparing his disciples for the postresurrection era, when he will not be physically with them to handle their problems as they were accustomed to him doing. They are now being launched into a life of prayer. They must learn to approach Almighty God themselves, through the Mediator, Jesus Christ.

## The Misunderstood Intercession of Christ

For the past fifty years, I have been engaged in intense personal discipling of individual Christians. I regularly ask people about their understanding of the intercession of Christ. Answers I receive range from incomplete to wrong. Here are samples of the exchanges.

Q: What activity do you picture Jesus engaged in right now?
A: I haven't thought much about that. *or*
A: Preparing a home for us. *or*
A: Praying for us.
Q: What does the expression "the intercession of Christ" bring to your mind?
A: Jesus is pleading our case before the Father.
Q: How do you relate the Lord's intercession to our praying?
A: He relays our requests to the Father and asks that they be granted.

The inadequacy of these responses will become evident as we proceed. Let's begin by returning to John 16:23-24. Notice that our Lord moves directly into additional statements that fit perfectly with what he has just said but contradict popular notions regarding his intercession. "In that day you will ask in my name. I am not saying that I will ask the Father on your behalf. No, the Father himself loves you because you have loved me and have believed that I came from God" (vv. 26-27).

The blessed alignment of prayer allows us to reach God directly by praying in Jesus Christ's name. What gets us through to the Father is that name, not any begging on Jesus' part. Read again verses 26 and 27 and be very sure your view of our Lord's intercession accords with Scripture.

The Roman Catholic practice of prayer can be like a chain with many links. Requests first go to saints and especially to Mary, who then seeks to persuade the Son, who then wins the Father's smile of approval. The popular Protestant view simply shortens the chain but has Jesus carry out the same function. In the two verses we are studying, however, Jesus seems to be saying that he will not be transferring to heaven the same go-between ministry that he performed on earth for the disciples. Before his death and resurrection, the disciples brought him their needs, and then he asked the Father on their behalf. In anticipation of his entrance into glory, however, Jesus says that this arrangement is to be changed. While believers might now come to him as God for the granting of their petitions, the basic, fundamental approach is that we stand on Christ's merit, in his name, and make known our desires directly to the Father.

The intercession of Christ, properly understood, does not have him receiving our requests and then passing them on to the Father, adding some sort of vocal leverage. Rather, Jesus presents *himself* before his Father, appearing there on our behalf. He ever lives to make this kind of intercession and advocacy with the Father. He is not begging and pleading, for his blood has propitiated the Father. The Father is satisfied. Jesus is seated in honor at the right hand of God. We do our own praying to the Father—only it must be in the name of the Christ in glory.

I hasten to add, "The Spirit helps us in our weakness. We do not know what we ought to pray for, but the Spirit himself intercedes for us with groans that words cannot express. And he who searches our hearts knows the mind of the Spirit, because the Spirit intercedes for the saints in accordance with God's will" (Rom. 8:26-27).

Praying is strengthened if the distinction between the intercession of Jesus and that of the Spirit is understood. Jesus intercedes in heaven at God's right hand. The Spirit intercedes within us. Jesus presents himself on our behalf. The Spirit assists us in presenting our requests acceptably, in manner and content. The Son gives us the authority of his name and his redemptive work. The Spirit helps us do the actual praying. If we form and present our petitions in accord with the Spirit, he will help us stand in Jesus Christ as we pray. Indeed, the biblical phrases "in the Spirit" and "in Christ" convey us into this very alignment. The two expressions are not synonymous. The first is inward in its area of activity, while the second is objective, before God. The Spirit conducts us along the path of proper praying, especially when we reach the end of our tether and we lack the insight or strength to pray as we should. Then Christ grants us the privilege and the right to approach God's throne with confidence. He stands *there* for us.

The misunderstood intercession of Christ generally conceives of our Lord's intercession as something supplementary to his propitiation. In fact, however, Christ's intercession is the implementation of the whole thrust of redemption, which the Book of Hebrews makes very clear. In 4:14-16 we are taught that our Great High Priest's identity with us in his past humiliation and now in his exaltation in glory above must strengthen our faith and provide the basis for our confident approach to God. The familiar words of 7:25, "he always lives to intercede," must not be lifted from their context and made to apply to Christ's

117

handling of the prayer traffic from all believers. Rather, in this passage he is being contrasted with other priests, whose ministry was so limited because of death—"because Jesus lives forever, he has a permanent priesthood" (v. 24). Finally, Jesus' ongoing intercession has to do with the power and accomplishment of his once-for-all sacrifice for our sins, in contrast with the struggle of earlier priests caught in endlessly repeating cycles of sacrifices. Jesus is forever positioned with the Father and seated in the place of honor and favor, representing us. See Hebrews 10:11-12.

Consider how sufficient this arrangement is. Whenever we might buckle under the weight and discipline of praying or fail in getting to the real issue of a need, the Holy Spirit is at hand to assist us. No evil-spirit confusion will overwhelm us if we rely on our Helper in prayer. At times, every believer will experience strong, even severe, accusations from Satan as prayer is attempted. Judas Iscariot, while under the devil's mastery, did not hesitate to disrupt the sanctity of Gethsemane and confront Jesus. Prayer, therefore, might bring us into spiritual conflict before delivering us from it. The ultimate answer to the enemy's accusations and belittlement is our appropriation of (that is, our seeing clearly and claiming confidently) the Savior's position of intercession on our behalf. If we have in fact sinned, we must turn to Jesus Christ as our Advocate. He is not our adversary. Satan is.

First John 2:1 teaches, "My dear children, I write this to you so that you will not sin. But if anybody does sin, we have one who speaks to the Father in our defense—Jesus Christ, the Righteous One." Incidentally, I do not feel it is necessary to introduce the notion of a verbal speaking in the translation of this text. That idea is not literally in the Greek and does not fit as well with the next verse. What is promised to the challenged prayer warrior is an advocacy by Christ that involves who he is and what he renders as our High Priest. Verse 2 explains that the Advocate himself is the propitiation for our sins: "He is the atoning sacrifice for our sins."

See how this role fits with Jesus' words, looked at earlier, in John 16:26-27. The advocacy of Christ is not burdened with having to convince a reluctant Father. Rather, Jesus was raised from the dead, and he was welcomed into glory and seated at the Father's right hand—all guaranteeing that the way is opened for us to make a confident approach to the Father, who truly loves us, for his Son's sake. The advocacy of Jesus Christ is the Father's porch light shining a welcome to his children.

## Table Talk That Makes My Point

The urgent need to clarify our Lord's mediation to those who would pray effectively was emphasized to me as I was composing this very section. At table with several friends, we began a discussion of 1 Corinthians 15:20-28. My friends' effort to understand the personal pronouns "he," "his," and "him" in this passage disclosed a deep confusion. "Who is putting what under whom?" they asked. I sought to help here by directing attention to verse 27, where it is made clear that the Father is bringing everything into subjection to Christ. This key can then be applied to the other verses in question.

A much deeper concern of mine, however, was the general vagueness among all the guests with reference to our Lord himself—as to his present personal condition and occupation. Now these friends were, to my mind, well above average in their depth of spiritual perception. Yet in their interpretation of the text, they emphasized the Father's relation with the Son within the Trinity.

Primarily, however, the text speaks about God and his

relation to the Son as incarnate man and as Christ our Mediator and Representative. Notice that the messianic title is used at the outset of the passage (v. 20), which is followed by: "For since death came through a man, the resurrection of the dead comes also through a man. For as in Adam all die, so in Christ all will be made alive" (vv. 21-22). What is being taught here is not the place of the Son in the Godhead but the scope of his position as the incarnate Mediator. This glorious section of Scripture is also telling us of our Lord's *present* rule and how the final state of eternal governance of the entire universe will be carried out. The One now exalted on the throne, while earth's rebellion is being ended, is our Head, and we are his own people and body. "In his name" we approach our God and his Father with our prayers, and in this way we share in the subjugation of evil.

Back away from all these details for a moment and consider what drives sincere believers to miss the revelation in this passage about Jesus' present rule. Many desire to see that our Lord Jesus "gets his due" and is released from his ties to us mortals and is subsumed back into a "Deity-only" condition. Such a view, though, would separate our Lord from us! Perhaps you, dear readers, will not be prepared to identify with this view, but maybe you would agree that many believers today are stifled in their prayer life by a very cloudy, unclear view of our Lord as he now is, this very moment, while they are praying in his name. These confusions will reduce a believer only to muttering the words "in his name" at the conclusion of another lifeless prayer. Such prayers do not seem to be offered through a heavenly Representative, who succeeded where Adam failed. Jesus, however, is now "both Lord and Christ" (Acts 2:36), and believers have the authority of his name as they pray.

Standing before our Father in prayer lays this absolute

requirement on us if we would succeed: we must have a clear understanding of Christ's *mediation* and his *intercession* for us. Clarifying these two terms will raise our spiritual level. Though related, the two terms are not identical in their emphasis. Consider each one briefly.

As Mediator, Christ uniquely connects us to his Father in heaven. Jesus both represents God to us and represents us before God. Accordingly Scripture says, "There is one God and one mediator between God and men, the man Christ Jesus" (1 Tim. 2:5). Emerging from the womb into our world, Jesus images God to us. As the incarnate Word, he expresses God's person and message to us. Then he mediates a new covenant. Next, see how our Mediator also represents us to God, for the next verse of this passage adds, "who gave himself as a ransom for all men" (v. 6).

As to Christ's intercession, the Book of Hebrews makes it clear that Jesus' triumphant entrance into heaven displays both the powerful authority given him as King of all and also his priestly intercession for us as he presents a perfect, once-for-all sacrifice for us. Blessings of this divine governance in my personal realm and of his priestly ministry for me personally will shower down upon my heart only to the extent that I see that the Lord Jesus Christ is my Mediator before God. The One who came from above to represent God to us has now gone from earth to represent us to God: "He entered heaven itself, now to appear *for us* in God's presence" (Heb. 9:24).

The wonderful point is that Christ's humanity continues. He is not released from us, but we are to be raised with him. All authority is in the hand of him who is "one of us." Prayers prevail as they are offered through this headship.

121

## Confidence in Prayer

If our doctrines regarding Christ are clear and firm, our prayers will be strong and confident. Prayer vitality is maintained not so much by knowing the fine points about praying as it is by knowing truth about Christ and how to align ourselves with him. Consider the powerful reason why this statement is true. Jesus taught, "But the Counselor, the Holy Spirit, whom the Father will send in my name, will teach you all things and will remind you of everything I have said" (John 14:26); "he will bring glory to me by taking from what is mine and making it known to you" (16:14). When the Spirit has his way with us, we will perceive Christ as now positioned in supreme authority and as available to see that prayer is answered. When these truths are allowed to dim, however, the Spirit of truth is grieved, and we lose his essential help in our praying. See Romans 8:26-27.

Effective prayer that prevails with God requires the Holy Spirit's very personal assistance. How else can we experience the rich depths of Hebrews 10:35-36? "So do not throw away your confidence; it will be richly rewarded. You need to persevere so that when you have done the will of God, you will receive what he has promised." This text gives fair warning that our understanding, our "doing," and our prayer within the will of God are not all there is to receiving "what he has promised." Check the verses again and realize that there might be a significant time gap between our prayerful obedience and the gracious answer. In that gap we are to endure in steady confidence. Hence, we need the Spirit to guide us (using Scripture) so that our prayers are on target, and also we need the Spirit to strengthen us in the discipline of endurance.

## The Scope of Prayer

Having to place ourselves consciously in Christ whenever we pray keeps us in our place and helps us see Christ in his place. How else could we be permitted to handle so great a trust of authority? The amount of truth about the Lord Jesus Christ that we possess will set the bounds on the exercise of our authority in prayer. Furthermore, the Holy Spirit will give his personal supervision and assistance to each faithful intercessor.

The scope of prayer responsibility is vast indeed, but it is a bounded authority. Our prayer life is connected to the administration of Jesus on the throne. We see him wearing the crown and wielding the scepter where Adam failed to exercise dominion. Through the Scripture and the illumination of the Holy Spirit, God makes known his secrets to his servants who pray. For example, God made known to Abraham the impending destruction of Sodom, and this information enabled Abraham, in turn, to intercede with God. We see the dramatic result of this prayer partnership between the Almighty and Abraham as Lot is rescued:

> Early the next morning Abraham got up and returned to the place where he had stood before the LORD. He looked down toward Sodom and Gomorrah, toward all the land of the plain, and he saw dense smoke rising from the land, like smoke from a furnace.
>
> So when God destroyed the cities of the plain, he remembered Abraham, and he brought Lot out of the catastrophe that overthrew the cities where Lot had lived. (Gen. 19:27-29)

The promise to the disciples of "greater things" (John 14:12) is immediately tethered to prayer and next to the promised Spirit of truth. Be assured that the Spirit of truth will keep the disciple tied to the Scriptures that he inspired.

Prayer's far-reaching domain is made clear to us in several Scriptures: "All authority in heaven and on earth has been given to me," says Jesus in Matthew 28:18. In Revelation 5 Jesus is portrayed as the only one in heaven or earth with the right to take the scroll from God's right hand and loose its seals. The breaking of each seal launches another major providential happening over the earth—but not without the prayers of faithful believers. The power and place of the saints' prayers are introduced at crucial junctures in the process of the Lord's opening the seals (Rev. 5:8 and 8:1-5).

Again, we are told in the familiar Romans 8:28 that God works in all things with reference to his purpose. This word is preceded by the promise of the Holy Spirit's assistance to those who in weakness do not know what to pray for (v. 26), but the Spirit's help is "in accordance with God's will" (v. 27). God's providence and our prayers are inextricably linked.

It is immediately obvious that only those fully committed to Christ will be entrusted with such responsibility. "The end of all things is near. Therefore be clear minded and self-controlled so that you can pray" (1 Peter 4:7). Inability to get through to God with large petitions very often results from a cluttered mind and lack of discipline. Two modern pitfalls are television and the Internet, whose excesses fatten the body but weaken the spirit.

## The Discipline of Trials
Substantial testing either erodes faith or strengthens it. The right kind of praying makes both mind and heart receptive to the elements of spiritual pruning and discipline that often are involved in our trials. Our Father in heaven is like an earthly parent who from the window keeps check on the children at play.

Some incidents of trouble will be witnessed but not immediately responded to. Every child must learn to go through difficulties. Wise parents will choose the response that is most advantageous to their child. Hopefully, the tearful little one will soon understand and trust.

Maturity, however, does not turn prayer into a smooth sail. Some requests must be persistently presented until faith is severely tested. The apostle Paul told the Colossians that prayer involves a struggling (Col. 2:1) and a wrestling (4:12). Furthermore, he urged the Thessalonians to "pray continually" (1 Thess. 5:17).

Nowhere in the Bible, then, is faith portrayed as a means of locking God into a mechanical system of cogwheel certainty. Ultimate outcomes are reserved for his hand to control. As we gain spiritual insight from God's Word and grow in experience, however, we taste more frequently the special joy of answered prayer. Humbling burdens and personal testing keep us teachable and lead us on to maturity.

## Insights

Here is a list of insights that have come to me as I have practiced prayer.

- Take time to focus the mind on God, with our Lord Jesus Christ at his right hand. Pray in the name of Christ, as we earlier discussed.
- Make your approach in response to Jesus' numerous invitations (examples: Matt. 7:7-11; John 14:13-14 and 15:7). Recite these verses, along with other Bible promises, as you present your petitions.
- See that all your requests are for the Father's ultimate glory, as John 14:13 and 15:8 indicate.
- Allow God to be in charge and do things his way, yet maintain

a persistent, prevailing attitude of confidence, mixed with a proper reverence.

- Learn to pray according to what is promised in Scripture, rather than how things seem. Consider how it must have seemed to the Canaanite woman in Matthew 15 when Jesus at first "did not answer a word," and next he gave her what apparently was a stinging refusal. Then put yourself in the shoes of the man outside the closed door, as pictured by Jesus in Luke 11. The poor fellow needs help, but what he hears from inside is, "Don't bother me. . . . I can't get up and give you anything." In the story in Luke 18 of the widow who overcomes the stubborn refusal of a mean official and gains a request, Christ's aim is made unmistakable. Luke says the parable is to show the disciples "that they should always pray and not give up." This divine dealing with intercessors is calculated to soften brashness, humble pride, and stretch weak spiritual muscles. Consider one last example, that of Mary and Martha, whose message to Jesus urged him to come to them because Lazarus, "the one you love," was sick (John 11:3). Then verses 5 and 6 add, "Jesus loved Martha and her sister and Lazarus. Yet when he heard that Lazarus was sick, he stayed where he was two more days." What was in the Lord's heart can be grasped only by faith, not by how it seems. This love bursts forth in response to each of the cases cited as the petitioner holds on.

- Appreciate the variety in the pattern of God's way of responding to us, always aiming at our good and our training in faith. Here is a list compiled from my experiences of the varying ways God works in answer to prayer.

  1. With startling immediacy—at times, right as one is praying.

2. After delays, and then at the last possible moment.
3. What seems to be a refusal. Yet the needs are still cared for, though not as expected or as desired. Learning to let God be God and to have unconditional trust is indeed a valuable lesson. Thoughtful interaction with the Father through striving in prayer is how we learn many deeper spiritual lessons.
4. A refusal with no alternative solutions provided. If properly received by the one praying, faith will be strengthened, and providence will not appear to contradict texts that plainly declare, "You ask and you get." True as these statements are, they do not mean that God has abandoned his personal participation as sovereign and senior in the partnership of prayer.
5. An ominous no response, with things getting worse—much worse. Mounting troubles engulf the heart in a blackness. All hope seems lost. Every escape route is blocked. Nor can one discern any possible profit from the wrenching and pounding experiences. In this extremity, many a weeping saint begins to sense the warmth of God's special presence. Finally, in the desperate darkness, the Father's choicest gift becomes discernable, but only by degrees. It is the jewel of a purified love for him, rarefied and known only to those who patiently endure heavy affliction. Now they know more than words can tell.

Such divine dealings are invaluable and perfectly calculated to keep us alive to God, as we are kept from the human tendency to reduce prayer to a mechanical system. A generation ago, conveniently placed coin-operated gumball machines invited us to punch in a coin; no need to wait for a clerk. As soon as the lever dropped in the money, an "answer" was on its way to our waiting palm. We could hear and see it coming. God's child, however, must not avoid deep, meaningful dealings with the Store Owner. Perseverance will be required, or confidence will fade. Thus each "refusal" is God's investment in our higher good. Perhaps something in the situation about which we are praying is not known to us, or a need exists in ourselves that God must meet, or maybe God wants more of our undivided attention. James 1:3-4 gives this insight: "You know that the testing of your faith develops perseverance. Perseverance must finish its work so that you may be mature and complete, not lacking anything." The only question is, Will faith flourish under this discipline, or will the intercessor shrink from the field and join the swollen ranks of those who quit?

## Finally and Simply

In prayer we practice God's presence and share in extending his providence. This relationship, like a good marriage, needs both daily investment and also the fostering of special times of extra attention—like arising at night to express love and worship, or setting aside selected hours or periods of time devoted to fasting and prayer. Each time Scripture is read, ask, How does this passage impact my praying? or What is God saying here that I should turn into prayer? Finally, prayer is simply the way of living by faith, walking in the Spirit, and getting on with God.

# 9

# BRIDGING TWO CREATIONS BY PROCLAMATION

"In the past God spoke to our forefathers through the prophets at many times and in various ways, but in these last days he has spoken to us by his Son" (Heb. 1:1-2). "This salvation, which was first announced by the Lord, was confirmed to us by those who heard him" (Heb. 2:3). "He has committed to us the message of reconciliation. We are therefore Christ's ambassadors, as though God were making his appeal through us. We implore you on Christ's behalf: Be reconciled to God" (2 Cor. 5:19-20).

Consider the sheer magnitude of this mission of continuing what our Lord "began to do" (Acts 1:1). The apostle Paul testifies of his own awakening to this calling. It involves, as he explains in 2 Corinthians 5:16-21, a totally new way of looking at Christ and other human beings. All who believe the redeeming message are moved from the old creation to the new. The one who goes forth to proclaim this saving truth stands, in all reality, between the two creations and directs those of this old world to change realms, to change their lineage from Adam's fallen line to that of their new Head, Jesus Christ.

The Christian witness who gives a gospel proclamation must ever be held in the grip of this colossal calling. It will determine our objectives. It also will set the content of the message and even how we speak. These matters must not be controlled by things of the old order, or old creation, but by things of the new. Here, then, is our great challenge: How can the preacher, standing as a tie-point between two so very different realms, properly connect with each?

If indeed "the god of this age has blinded the minds of unbelievers, so that they cannot see the light of the gospel of the glory of Christ, who is the image of God" (2 Cor. 4:4), then how can this blackness be penetrated? If unbelievers are "dead in . . . transgressions and sins [and are following] the ways of this world and of the ruler of the kingdom of the air, the spirit who is now at work in those who are disobedient" (Eph. 2:1-2), and if "they are darkened in their understanding and separated from the life of God because of the ignorance that is in them due to the hardening of their hearts" (Eph. 4:18)—then it surely follows that no human means is sufficient to reach into and change such hearts.

To overcome all these obstacles, the Lord's witness must, first of all, be true to the One who has commissioned and sent him. Second, the preacher must both gain a hearing and be understood with clarity and power—with such power as to wrench hearers from the grasp of Satan and the world and to bring about their forgiveness and transformation into the new creation. Only God can possibly accomplish such a change. The apostle is very clear in his testimony about the scope of this very reorientation: "For he has rescued us from the dominion of darkness and brought us into the kingdom of the Son he loves, in whom we have redemption, the forgiveness of sins" (Col. 1:13-14).

## God's Answer to the Impossible Quandary

Imagine this assignment: march boldly into a local cemetery, take your stand among the graves, and proclaim life to the dead. A staggering task! Even more so if you are told to stay at your post until there is a movement out of the graves and into life among the town's citizens. In truth, this is our assignment as Christians. How are we managing?

In the face of such impossibilities, we cry out with the disciples, "Who then can be saved?" And Jesus responds, "With man this is impossible, but with God all things are possible" (Matt. 19:25-26).

We have appraised that which overchallenges our gospel proclamation. Now let us measure the magnitude of the divine, mighty resources given us for making the "impossible" possible. Consider four of these resources:

1. *Authority directly from the Lord Jesus Christ.* He said, "All authority in heaven and on earth has been given to me. Therefore go and make disciples of all nations, baptizing them in the name of the Father and of the Son and of the Holy Spirit, and teaching them to obey everything I have commanded you. And surely I am with you always, to the very end of the age" (Matt. 28:18-20).

2. *Power of the Holy Spirit.* "But you will receive power when the Holy Spirit comes on you; and you will be my witnesses . . . to the ends of the earth" (Acts 1:8). "When he comes, he will convict the world of guilt in regard to sin and righteousness and judgment" (John 16:8).

3. *Profundity and strength of the message we proclaim.* The gospel message is "that Christ died for our sins according to the Scriptures, that he was buried, that he was raised on the third day according to the Scriptures, and that he

131

appeared" (1 Cor. 15:1-5). "Repentance and forgiveness of sins will be preached in his name to all nations" (Luke 24:47). "The gospel . . . is the power of God for the salvation of everyone who believes" (Rom. 1:16).

4. *Prayer.* "And pray . . . that God may open a door for our message, so that we may proclaim the mystery of Christ. . . . Pray that I may proclaim it clearly, as I should" (Col. 4:3-4). "Finally, brothers, pray for us that the message of the Lord may spread rapidly and be honored" (2 Thess. 3:1).

## Man's Way Won't Work

Trying to persuade those perishing in their sin to be reconciled to God and to come into life can be a daunting undertaking. This difficulty drives us to "persuade" God in prayer to please bless our efforts. Standing there between the two worlds, our attention is more and more drawn to the realm of the most "noise." Without waiting to be clothed with God's power and full directions, we are habitually drawn into action and "ministry," using our own strengths and contrivances.

Our prayers may ascend more or less regularly, beseeching divine blessings on the efforts we employ. Prayer, however, often takes second place to public relations. Publicity and marketing skills are now deeply embedded in the mission of proclamation. Once the emphasis has shifted from dealing with God on behalf of mankind to that of dealing with men and women on behalf of God, communication barriers then mire the preacher in all kinds of bogs. Modernity itself is a many-faced obstacle. Barriers that are cultural, generational, and societal add to the burden.

In contrast with the inexplicably mysterious growth of a planted, living seed, the results of even the most masterful of contrivances can be explained. Thoughtful amazement overtakes us when we consider how the tiny kernel germinates, roots, sprouts, and produces perhaps a hundredfold. But much of the church's ingathering today can be explained in terms of skillfully directed programs and even the talent of the chief spokesperson. So many ergs of energy on the input side, and so much fruit results on the output.

When one ceases to rely on laws of life and turns to human resources, the entire battle plan is altered. For example, "Something for All Ages" is a slogan that churches frequently use in their advertising. It is well and good to provide for people of all ages, but we must ask whether the motto means more than that. Is it not in many minds that the "foolishness of preaching" and public family worship are not captivating enough to hold everyone's attention? If so, then we are on track to discovering our problem. Let's not compound our plight by turning away from the power of the Holy Spirit to vitalize the preaching and worship of the church, and to stir and convince those outside the fold of salvation.

We have an indication of the wrong tack in gospel proclamation when the public prayers seem detached from God and when the preaching seems very attached to the world. In an effort to communicate effectively, many reach for the wrong resources. What is sometimes referred to as "working the audience" is an expression of this orientation. Inordinate amounts of humor and techniques designed to stir up the emotions become essential. We frequently hear phrases such as "Watch this now!" (as if the message almost involves some kind of sleight of hand) or "Stay with me now, and I will break it down for you." Even if no pride is present on the preacher's part, such expressions might involve an overemphasis on trying to reach listeners from the outside, rather than having confidence that God's Spirit is working within the hearts of all who hear.

## God's Way Works

Paul the apostle said, "The gospel I preached is not something that man made up. I did not receive it from any man, nor was I taught it; rather, I received it by revelation from Jesus Christ" (Gal. 1:11-12). Peter made it clear that the center of the message is Jesus: "Salvation is found in no one else, for there is no other name under heaven given to men by which we must be saved" (Acts 4:12).

Representing God and presenting this gospel is an overwhelming assignment because "Jews demand miraculous signs and Greeks look for wisdom, but we preach Christ crucified: a stumbling block to Jews and foolishness to Gentiles" (1 Cor. 1:22-23). None of these obstacles, however, moved Paul to alter his proclamation:

> When I came to you, brothers, I did not come with eloquence of superior wisdom as I proclaimed to you the testimony about God. For I resolved to know nothing while I was with you except Jesus Christ and him crucified. I came to you in weakness and fear, and with much trembling. My message and my preaching were not with wise and persuasive words, but with a demonstration of the Spirit's power, so that your faith might not rest on men's wisdom, but on God's power. (1 Cor. 2:1-5)

Though in their blindness the people of this world "crucified the Lord of glory" (1 Cor. 2:8), the apostle Paul is confident that the Holy Spirit can open hearts to receive the gospel message: "As it is written: 'No eye has seen, no ear has heard, no mind has conceived what God has prepared for those who love him'—but

God has revealed it to us by his Spirit" (vv. 9-10).

Fallen men are like grounded wet leaves, matted and difficult to rake, but the wind that helps the sun dry them soon moves them along. When prayer prevails in faith, the same Spirit that brings men and women down in repentance from their lofty branches can move them into God's family. Devising better techniques of moving matted masses is not what is needed. Apart from direct help from God, how can the witness express what is "indescribable" (2 Cor. 9:15) so effectively that sinful rebels are drawn into a personal encounter with the One whose truth and ways are beyond discovery (Rom. 11:33)?

Putting it more specifically, we believers are sent out to convince unbelievers, who have never seen anyone rise from the dead, that Jesus is alive. Then we are to help them as newborn children of God to love and bond with the Savior, whom they have never seen (1 Peter 1:8).

We have two obvious lessons to learn and practice. First, our own capacities and approaches are insufficient for effective gospel proclamation. Second, God can and will empower the proclamation once we lay aside our dependence on "props" and pray and preach as we ought.

## Looking More Deeply at Today's Church Scene

"Win them by joining them" seems to be the watchword of many in the contemporary church. By befriending the world, however, one becomes the enemy of God, as James 4:4 warns: "You adulterous people, don't you know that friendship with the world is hatred toward God? Anyone who chooses to be a friend of the world becomes an enemy of God" (see also Phil. 3:18-19). How, then, are we to get across our message if "the god of this age has blinded the minds of unbelievers, so that they cannot see the light of the gospel of the glory of Christ, who is the image of God" (2 Cor. 4:4)?

In shocking contrast with so much of today's stress on public relations, consider the approach of John the Baptist. His clothing and appearance were crude, his location was inconvenient, and his message was blunt: "And so John came, baptizing in the desert region and preaching a baptism of repentance for the forgiveness of sins. The whole Judean countryside and all the people of Jerusalem went out to him. Confessing their sins, they were baptized by him in the Jordan River. John wore clothing made of camel's hair, with a leather belt around his waist, and he ate locusts and wild honey" (Mark 1:4-6).

Jesus and his apostles faced many problems, but never the problem of how to stir up interest and gain a hearing. "He could not keep his presence secret" (Mark 7:24); unconcern was not an issue. When "crowds of people came to hear him," Jesus "often withdrew to lonely places and prayed" (Luke 5:15-16). So also Paul repeatedly sought to enlist others to help gain a hearing for the gospel through their prayers (see, for example, Col. 4:3). The question needs to be faced frankly: Have we today turned from strong crying to God in prayer for our generation and, instead, focused on attracting people by our own wisdom and gimmicks?

Often those driven to impress people are themselves too much impressed by people. Underlying this controlling drive is really what Scripture condemns as the fear of man. God's word to Jeremiah was, "Get yourself ready! Stand up and say to them whatever I command you. Do not be terrified by them, or I will terrify you before them" (Jer 1:17). Undoubtedly, the intimidating challenge to communicate with, and relate to, the varied lot of modern humanity leads many to stress method above the essence of the message and the might of prayer.

There was definitely a "gap" between the Roman governor Felix and the shackled Jewish prisoner Paul, who stood before him. The encounter, though, clearly evidenced the Holy Spirit's blessing on the apostle's proclamation of truth, as recorded in Acts 24:24-25: Felix "sent for Paul and listened to him as he spoke about faith in Christ Jesus. As Paul discoursed on righteousness, self-control and the judgment to come, Felix was afraid and said, 'That's enough for now! You may leave.'" This powerful shaking of a hardened official's heart was not accomplished by any fabricated method of communication. Rather, Paul was simply one of those who "preached the gospel . . . by the Holy Spirit sent from heaven" (1 Peter 1:12).

Paul made it clear to the Corinthians that he was sent by Christ "to preach the gospel—not with words of human wisdom, lest the cross of Christ be emptied of its power" (1 Cor. 1:17). "My message and my preaching were not with wise and persuasive words, but with a demonstration of the Spirit's power" (2:4). He also reminded the Thessalonians, "Our gospel came to you not simply with words, but also with power, with the Holy Spirit and with deep conviction" (1 Thess. 1:5).

Whenever the gospel is presented, the encounter should be a dynamic one, marked with three evidences of God's power:

1. The enemy Satan is confronted and defeated.
2. Unbelievers are confronted and convinced.
3. The Holy Spirit is received by those who believe what they hear.

Admittedly, some will see the above as mere theoretical idealism. Not so. Instead, it is what Scripture promises. The contrast between what Scripture says and what experience shows today is a solemn testimony to the urgency of our theme in this book.

CRUCIAL PRACTICES NOW WEAKENED

## Where Did the Power Go?

Our loss of the Spirit's power is not directly the result of our failure to come up with better ways of connecting with contemporary society. No, we are perhaps driven to seek new methods of relating to our hearers because the power is already missing, and our Lord may be withholding his blessings because he is grieved. The grieving could occur because his message is being altered or "adjusted."

Many of these contemporary alterations to our proclamation have something in common: they avoid making the demand for repentance, unlike the practice of John the Baptist, Jesus, and the apostles (Mark 1:4, 14-15; Acts 2:38). This avoidance is seen in the following familiar instances:

1. When the gospel invitation is extended and hearers are urged to "let Jesus in" or to "accept Christ into your heart and life." Although these familiar expressions are not in themselves wrong, the problem arises when those who are not in God's family are given the impression that they may enter the fold without a true repentance for their sins and a submission to Jesus Christ as their new Lord. Those in Adam's lineage are perishing unless they find a new headship in Jesus Christ and are regenerated and born anew.

2. When the evangelistic message is aimed at changing hearers' thinking from holding that salvation is "by works" to agreeing that salvation is "by grace." While the first viewpoint must be changed, yet merely adopting the right opinion will not necessarily remove the element of sinful pride. Some who have not been convinced by the Holy Spirit of their sin and jeopardy before the almighty Judge do in fact assent to the gospel presentation and determine to follow the Christian way. Again, in these cases, repentance is missing; it is not a part of the equation

because the cross has not been given its place.

3. When it is declared that Jesus died on the cross as our substitute but the nature of the substitution is not made clear. His suffering and death were more than paying a price for our many sins, but the way in which he substitutes himself in our place is very significant. Jesus stands officially, legally in the stead of the fallen sinner, as the Last Adam, taking the full curse of Adam's lot on himself there on the cross. Then he rises from the dead to represent believers as Head of their new lineage and thus enables us to stand before God as justified, now newborn from the dead.

Careful reflection will again make it evident that, in the light of Jesus' full substitution for us, gospel repentance must be deep and profound. Yes, we have indeed sinned against God and broken his laws, but even more, we can never measure up to divine standards because we are part of an accursed human family. Rather than attempting to measure up to God's requirements, we must see on Calvary's cross the spectacle of what we deserve, there in the form of our dying Substitute. This view leads to a lifetime posture of repentance and a continual drawing upon the Spirit's power to deal with our inner proneness to sin.

Jesus Christ warns us, "Unless you repent, you too will all perish" (Luke 13:3). When the apostle Paul gave the Ephesian elders a solemn review of his ministry among them, he said, "I have declared to both Jews and Greeks that they must turn to God in repentance and have faith in our Lord Jesus" (Acts 20:21). The linkage between repentance and faith is indissoluble. Apart from faith in Jesus Christ, full repentance is impossible. Apart from repentance, faith in Jesus Christ is impossible. Seeing what I truly am drives me to the Savior. Conversely, committing myself to this One "who had no sin" but was made "to be sin for us" (2 Cor. 5:21) will be concurrent with correct self-appraisal. As 2 Peter 3:9 puts it, God wants "everyone to come to repentance."

## How Much Do the Newborn Know?

What is the minimal knowledge level for those who come for salvation? How much truth must be known in order for one to be saved? Admittedly, it is not necessary to place before hearers all the distinctions we have been discussing each time the gospel is preached. It is necessary, however, that the one giving God's Word have the foundation stones squarely set in his or her own understanding so as to make a certain impact of power. The new believers in Rome did not yet know all the truths that the apostle discussed in that epistle, but he did not allow them to stay in the shallows. The very writing of that grand epistle proves that God intends for us all to "grow in the grace and knowledge of our Lord and Savior Jesus Christ" (2 Peter 3:18).

The basic issue in personal salvation is the element of surrender located in repentance toward God and faith in Christ. Once the Spirit convinces a person of sin and lostness, the will must be yielded over to God: "If only you will receive me— unworthy as I am, Lord—I come to you." Such an attitude is prelude to genuine salvation. Then the way is cleared for laying hold of Christ's payment for sin.

## Final Words

Many new believers do not know, in depth, the truths that saved them. For such people, it is presumptuous to preach and teach only on the surface of things. Flat and shallow vessels with little draft are more easily blown off course.

A special phenomenon needs mentioning. Some experienced preachers have looked back over years of service and wondered why their earlier years of innocent ignorance were marked with a kind of fruitfulness unseen in their later ministry. Could it be that as they grew in experience, education, and responsibilities, their simple faith in God diminished? Learning better techniques of "handling" God's Word does not necessarily bring more power of the Spirit. Some preachers are like David in Saul's armor, better equipped, but unable to declare with a certain authority, "Thus saith the Lord!" Young David with only a sling and stones could face and defeat giant Goliath and say with assurance, "I come against you in the name of the LORD Almighty" (1 Sam. 17:45).

By now it should be obvious that our proclamation of the gospel, in both method and content, is largely shaped by the view we have of the truths covered in part 1. A painful example of the mishandling of key truths is seen in the number who preach and sing that there is "power in the blood," even while divine power seems to be missing. Great care is taken to label correctly each bottle of truth given to the thirsty, but the containers are often filled with the very content the preacher meant to reject. The cross is preached, but without propitiation being clearly laid down as the one basis for the forgiveness being proclaimed.

Flaws in the preaching are most often traceable to misunderstood truth, though the teacher may be largely unaware of the problem and may even feel doctrinally sound. To expose this hidden problem, readers are urged to take the test presented in appendix 6. There I attempt to demonstrate that many Christians often quote familiar atonement texts but seldom make reference to their context.

Beyond measure is the glorious honor given believers to share in the promulgation of the news of salvation. This salvation we proclaim must not be truncated into a trite mini-message of our own traditional way of looking at things. The salvation set forth in the songs and stories of the Old Testament, expounded in the

New Testament, and climaxed in Revelation begins with release from slavery of sin and extends to all the daily mercies, favors, and "marvelous things" (Ps. 98:1) that God does and gives along life's way, until he at last rescues us from this life and brings us into the eternal liberty of heaven. Furthermore, the dimensions of our proclamation extend to multitudes, called out of earth's nations and people groups and into God's vast chorus of salvation:

> Sing to the LORD, praise his name;
>> proclaim his salvation day after day.
> Declare his glory among the nations,
>> his marvelous deeds among all peoples.
>> (Ps. 96:2-3)

> Great and marvelous are your deeds,
>> Lord God Almighty.
> Just and true are your ways,
>> King of the ages.
> Who will not fear you, O Lord,
>> and bring glory to your name?
> For you alone are holy.
> All nations will come
>> and worship before you,
> for your righteous acts have been revealed.
>> (Rev. 15:3-4)

# 10

# DISCIPLESHIP COUNSELING

We are promised in the Bible that truth drawn from Scripture has the dynamic to teach, rebuke, correct, and train in righteousness. This is so because "all Scripture is God-breathed," and when properly used in counseling others, inspired truth will draw them to become "thoroughly equipped for every good work" (2 Tim. 3:16-17). If this grand text, buttressed with many similar ones, is taken seriously, then troubled persons will not quickly be sent outside the church for help. Concerning the multitude famished for food, Jesus admonished his disciples, "They do not need to go away. You give them something to eat" (Matt. 14:16). Jesus blessed what little bread and fish they had, and everyone's need was met.

My objective here is not to speak against making referrals to counseling specialists but to speak in favor of fellow believers bringing helpful truth to troubled persons, and doing so in the context of the church. Rarely are all the church's resources brought to bear on disturbed lives.

Before we go into detailed discussion of what discipleship counseling involves, I should make it clear that by "discipling," I mean everything that is included in 2 Timothy 3:16-17. This full-orbed training and upbuilding in the Christian life should both meet the needs of active believers and in turn prepare them to help others, even those who might be classified as troubled persons. All such ministry is within the scope of what I mean by discipleship counseling.

Here is a brief summation of the resources that ought to be employed in counseling people with distressing problems:

1. *The varied dimensions of grace available from God in the life of the suffering person.* Discouraged, distraught believers must be helped to clear away hindrances that might be in their life so as to see with freshness what Christ has done on their behalf. Proceed graciously at this point. Don't first lay duties on broken people; rather, tell them what has been done for them by the Savior. Next, help them to realize the Holy Spirit's assistance for taking corrective action.

2. *The potential resources of help from family members of the one in need.* The brokenness in a troubled life is frequently traceable to dysfunction in the home. It follows that, if the church's intervention is holistic enough to bring an influence of healing into the family, a root alteration will be brought to the problems at hand. In every case, effort should be made to reach and change other members of the family. They should be encouraged to share as far as possible in the process of recovery.

3. *The extensive, varied resources of the local church fellowship.* The picture should be that of the church fellowship surrounding all the family that surrounds the struggling individual. I have on occasion arranged to go to a home and meet with an entire family for counseling and prayer, using selected Scriptures. In addition, special counseling can be given to the husband and wife. Often major difficulties provide an ideal time to launch individual discipling with each family member. When such steps

are taken, family members cease being part of the problem and, instead, contribute to the solution.

In chapter 13 we will study the structure and life of the local church, but for now let us assume that we are speaking of an assembly of believers whose members are trained and equipped to be instruments of healing. Discovering and preparing such ministering ones requires more than congregational and small-group ministries. Individual discipling is essential. Only in this way can a believer's level of comprehension be ascertained and increased with certainty. Next, the individual's personal appropriation of essential truths must be addressed. A mere grasp of doctrinal facts is not enough. Finally, expression of truth must become a part of each believer's life. The development of these three spiritual dimensions—comprehension, appropriation, and expression—presents a fundamental pastoral challenge to each church. To meet this challenge, in the early years of my ministry I developed a series of guided discipling sessions that I call Spiritual Life Studies. These thirteen-week interactions between two individuals were intended also to be adapted for the edification of church leaders, members, and even new converts.

## Putting It All Together—an Example

Here is a true story that illustrates the value of integrating counseling and discipling. Life was completely disrupted—or, I might say, smashed—for Ronald and Sarah, a handsome, affluent couple in their prime years, just before an early retirement. Sarah was stricken with a rapidly progressing terminal cancer. Always the strong, energetic one, she was now emaciated and in such pain that she was barely able to move around in her house. When I visited the home, Sarah was realistic about what was ahead—days in bed relying on morphine to cope with the mounting pain, then death. She confided that the nights, with the excruciating pain, already were becoming a terror to them both.

Immediately, I perceived that reading Bible verses to her on the subject of comfort would be inadequate to sustain her through the long hours of struggle. I chose instead to employ a kind of discipleship counseling, hoping to bring a change that would continue within her permanently. She desperately needed equipping for her greatest-ever challenge.

It was apparent that Sarah had a personal faith in Jesus Christ, but her husband, Ronald, did not. A few questions quickly disclosed that her spiritual history had left her unprepared for what she faced. As I inwardly prayed for guidance, Sarah's need became obvious: she must gain a vital, more confident access to God in prayer to sustain her in the long hours of searing pain. Accordingly, on that first visit I determined to center everything on one issue: how does one truly pray in Jesus' name? I pressed her to put in plain words what that concept means. "Just saying the words 'in Jesus' name, Amen' is not enough," I explained.

"After all these years of closing prayers with those words, I must admit that I do not understand what I have been saying," was her frank admission. I was glad I had come, for here was one of God's children locked in a struggle with our last enemy, death, and very unprepared.

A new light came into her tired eyes as she realized in a fuller way the privilege of bringing her heavy load to the Father in heaven. Her faith mounted up as she clung to the new insight that her prayers—racked and rattled though they might be— were dear to the Father because they were presented in his Son's name, in his perfect merit. How she relished that truth, speaking of it (and practicing it) over and over again! "Now in the dark nights, I can stand before God and be heard!" she declared.

On my next visit there, I had in mind two objectives. My first one was to ask her, "Do you think of the Holy Spirit as a real person?" (I reasoned that she needed a very *personal* ministry of the Spirit.) After drawing out her thoughts, I discovered that regardless of what "doctrinal statement" she might personally have agreed to, she in fact did not conceive of the Spirit as a person.

Ignorance regarding the Holy Spirit seems to hamper or limit the Spirit's work within his children. To the extent that the ignorance is allowed to exist, something we might call a "willing ignorance" (see translations of 2 Peter 3:5 for this concept), the Spirit must surely be grieved. Regardless, my suffering friend was now eager to have the full assistance of God's Spirit, and she earnestly asked forgiveness for her careless neglect of this gracious person.

Now, with the Spirit helping her, the previous week's accent on prayer became even more meaningful. A light was now shining in her dark night. But more needed to be done. My second objective for this visit was to talk to her husband about his own spiritual life. Outside, with Bible open on the trunk of his Mercedes, I urged him to repent of sin and trust altogether in the Lord Jesus.

"I can't do that," he objected. "I know so little about God or the Bible. In fact, this is my first conversation like this in my entire life." That very evening, however, he uttered his first audible prayer—childlike, but genuine.

It now became possible to institute the holy alignment prescribed in 1 Corinthians 11:3, where God, Christ, man, and woman are related in a proper way: "Now I want you to realize that the head of every man is Christ, and the head of the woman is man, and the head of Christ is God."

"Beginning this very evening, you must help your wife with Scripture."

"Wait a moment!" he interrupted. "I know nothing about the Bible, and she has been at this for years."

"I quite understand that, but you are her husband, and God will bless what you share. He will help you do it. First tell her what you have done here with me. Then begin reading together through the Gospel of Mark, a portion each night."

Beside these visits with Sarah, I saw that she had edifying visits from others in the church, and I scheduled weekly discipling with Ronald, using my Spiritual Life Studies. The results of this investment were marvelous indeed. During the distressful nights "we now have something definite and helpful to do," they told me with joy. With Ronald's gentle but enthusiastic leadership, they read through book after book of the Bible until the end came. And so it was that counseling with truth was infused into a suffering person's life, hour after hour, right from within the home. How could weekly professional appointments match this?

Honoring her request that I try to be present when her hour of death came, I went to the hospital where she had been taken one afternoon and decided to stay through the night. She was still lucid, but I sensed that the end was near. Shortly before dawn, I rose from the uncomfortable waiting-room chairs and went again to my friend's room. Sitting there with her were her son and daughter, one on each side holding her hands. Her husband, Ronald, was at that moment rushing back to her room. I soon indicated to them that she was about to leave us. Close to her ear I whispered encouragement, and as she was dying, I read these words: "The time has come for my departure. I have fought the good fight, I have finished the race, I have kept the faith. Now there is in store for me the crown of righteousness, which the

Lord, the righteous Judge, will award to me on that day—and not only to me, but also to all who have longed for his appearing" (2 Tim. 4:6-8).

In a peaceful quiet, her body stilled. I then read the final words of the selected text again, applying them to Sarah's life and appealing to the son and daughter to place their faith in Christ. At that moment Ronald returned, and we all stood at the bedside for a final commitment.

Following the funeral, one thing remained. I continued weekly discipling sessions with Ronald. By the time the planned meetings were finished, he was functioning very well and continued on in his new faith.

I have related this account in some detail to show the strength and potential of our spiritual resources to help individuals in crisis. It is true that I, a pastor, took most of the initiatives here, but there were dozens of others in the church who could have done so, and some did share in this ministry. What I did was not because of professional position but simply because the need came to me and I chose to take it up myself. A properly equipped church has a company of men and women who know how to counsel, support, and disciple. In this story, notice how each of the three resources listed earlier came into play.

First, the wife and the husband were each, personally, cultivated spiritually. Next, they were moved forward in grace so that they might in turn minister to one another, and they were helped to reach out to their unreached children. Finally, my task also included the bringing of other ministering ones from our church fellowship into this home of need, so that all the resources we have been discussing were involved in the ministry to this family.

Discounting personality and emotional problems where

the ultimate root was organic, I do not recall ever seeing that a referral had to be made to professionals outside the church when all these resources were faithfully applied. A key to this full-orbed application of spiritual resources is the shepherding. The ailing sheep must not be expected to come for help at the shepherd's convenience. Sheep-needs are the shepherd's concern, which means that the shepherd will pursue the sheep, going into their homes. The troubled one is personally strengthened and taught to exercise his or her spiritual resources. Family members are helped individually, and the home is strengthened so as to become a place of healing. And the church family must be involved fully in it all.

## Foundations of Discipleship Counseling

At this point, I wish to highlight two important fundamentals bearing on counseling. I cite this pair because they are so crucial and so often not given their recognition and place. These two essentials are *the nature of God's Word*, as it is in Scripture, and *the nature of a human person*, including the one you might seek to counsel.

Our beginning point must be that God knows and cares about people with problems, that their difficulties are not beyond his wisdom and power to help. It would be unthinkable, then, that his Word would not speak to such a large segment of the world's population as represented by those suffering mental and emotional distress. Scripture is indeed not silent here.

However, if the doctrinal defects addressed in part 1 are allowed to stand, then divine help will be very limited. For example, an earnest Christian lady once came to see me with severe inner turmoil. I knew that in years gone by she had been a highly valued teacher in the church. Young children crowded her classes to learn the Bible. But here she was bowed and broken, finding no solace and strength in the things she once taught. After prayer for God's help and direction, this is how I proceeded:

"In your thinking, is the Holy Spirit the 'influence of God,' or is the Spirit a person?"

"Well, I know he is not a person like Jesus," she replied.

"True, he is not in a body as Jesus was, but is he really a person?" Finally, it came out that her view of God's Spirit was very nebulous and inadequate. Perhaps such a lack of understanding might be excusable in a new believer, but certainly not in a teacher. She was in dire need of special help from the Spirit of truth to encourage and enlighten her, but he was limited by her responsible ignorance. With cleared insights came a lifting of her spirit. I have seen others whose angry dispositions and passions were brought under control after clearing up this same truth about the Spirit.

Although additional discipleship counseling may well be needed in cases of this kind, no counseling will be fully effective in a believer's life if foundational truths are not straight. Discovering and rectifying any misunderstood biblical doctrine is a critical step in counseling. Once understood, that very truth becomes a key in the person's recovery. It is of the very nature of inscripturated truth to speak to the needs of humanity.

## Bodies Die, Persons Live

A second fundamental in counseling is the nature of a human person. Bodies do not make the person. (After all, nonpersonal creatures also have bodies.) The body might sicken and die, ending the relationship between the body and its spirit, but the personal spirit lives on. It is created in the image of God and is conscious, rational, moral, and volitional.

Even if life could be synthesized, that fabrication would be no more human than a soft-skinned computer. Any powered machine "eats" from its power supply and is dependent upon input from outside intellectual sources. A person also eats and has other external input, but essentially the person is in very nature a rational and volitional agent, capable of initiating, or generating, his or her own "input" by thinking, deciding, and then acting.

This ability, or capacity, to choose and initiate action is at the root of personhood. Proper counsel, then, must correctly employ truth (the first fundamental in discipleship counseling), and that counsel must engage and involve the will of the person. Good counsel must therefore aim at aligning the individual's will with the will of the Creator. We were made by and for God. If deviation from the laws of God is done in ignorance, without knowing God's will, then simple enlightenment is necessary. However, if God's "perfect law that gives freedom" (James 1:25) is violated with some degree of knowledge, recovery will require repentance and reconciliation with God.

A prevalent feeling exists that it is somehow cruel to assign responsibility for one's action. This view is so misguided! True, the counselor must always be most uncruel in manner, but it is dehumanizing to keep a person from sensing blame where it is warranted. In our real and fallen world, accountability necessarily involves blame. This accountability separates us from the amorality of the animal realm. This principle accords with Scripture, and I have seen it validated in experience over many years.

## Discovering Our Roots

We have arrived at an important point in our journey to *bring Christ back* as we seek to apply all that we have covered up to this point to troubled personalities. (See figure 2.) Mankind's major taproot of trouble is most assuredly our status as sinners before God. From our very conception into Adam's family, we are under condemnation. In some detail this point has been set

**The Troubled Personality**

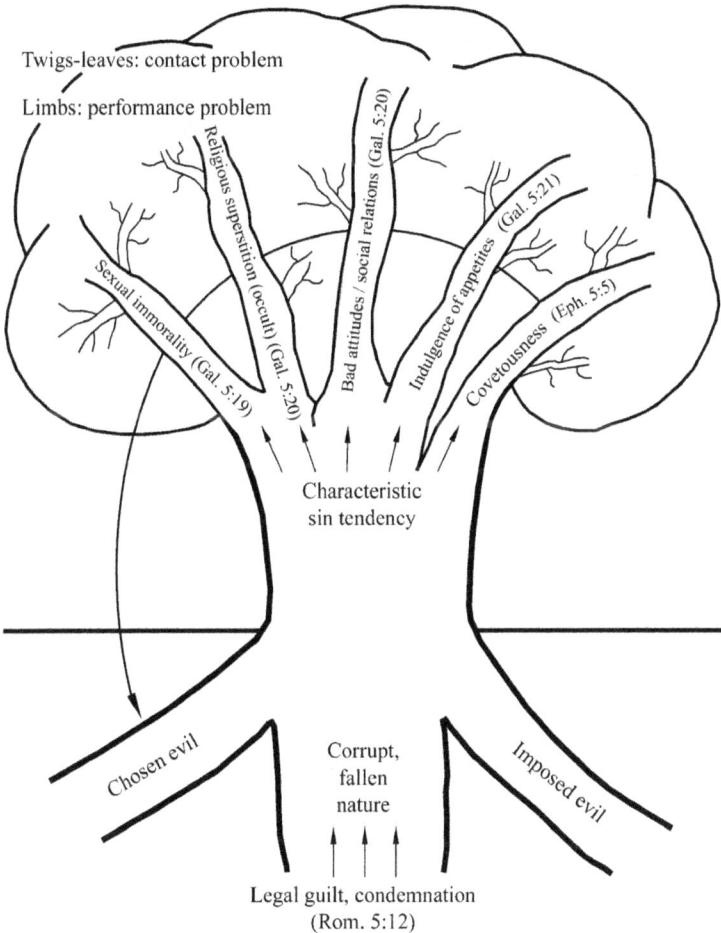

Twigs-leaves: contact problem
Limbs: performance problem
Religious superstition (occult) (Gal. 5:20)
Bad attitudes / social relations (Gal. 5:20)
Indulgence of appetites (Gal. 5:21)
Sexual immorality (Gal. 5:19)
Covetousness (Eph. 5:5)
Characteristic sin tendency
Chosen evil
Corrupt, fallen nature
Imposed evil
Legal guilt, condemnation (Rom. 5:12)

Figure 2

forth both in the text and in appendix 2, on the death of infants. Our guilt, inherited from Adam, brings the sentence of death, and though we might not face the grave for some years, the blight in our character is executed at once. From our beginning—to our very roots—we are corrupted and fallen in our nature, as figure 2 shows.

Besides the central taproot, human personality has two other determining roots: (1) the evil we individually choose as participants in sinful expression, and (2) all the evil that is contributed to, or imposed on, us. Through the first root, what we do contributes to our character; a sinful practice, if continued, will be a determining force in our lives. Through the second root, things outside our own choices—factors both genetic and environmental—have an impact on us. Those who give us birth and all who relate to us have a determining influence on us.

## Expressing Our Roots

All major forms of sinful expression are portrayed by the limbs in figure 2. I draw these from Scripture, exactly as they are listed in Galatians 5:19-21. The apostle gives them in related groups. First, he lists sins that are sexual in nature. Second, the terms "idolatry" and "witchcraft" have to do with superstition, the occult, or false religion. Third, the longest list is social or relational, having to do with attitudes and actions toward others. Fourth, the final expressions, "drunkenness, orgies, and the like," connote indulgence of sinful appetites. (To make this system of grouping evident, the NIV translators inserted semicolons to separate the four categories of sin in the Galatians 5 list.) I have added a fifth limb to the picture—greed, materialism, or covetousness, from Ephesians 5:5. To my mind, these five limbs stand for all the patterns of sinful expression that I have encountered in counseling.

Since sin is universal, it must be considered. Everyone has his or her own limbs of sinful tendencies. These limbs tend to grow and produce their fruit unless God's grace intervenes. Without that intervention, the harvest can be ruinous to lives. The size and shape of things above ground, so to speak, will depend on the various input from the roots and what is done about that input.

In other words, each person will have his or her own individual set of tendencies and weaknesses that will decide which limb or limbs are more prone to be sinfully active. The strength of one's inclinations is a product of one's own choices and deeds, plus birth input (genetics), combined with environmental input. Careful study and analysis of the five tree limbs in figure 2, together with the texts from which they are taken, will prove valuable in deciphering much of human behavior.

## Displaying or Covering Our Fruit

Human beings tend to grow their own system of branches, and also to produce the twigs and leaves to display what they want seen and to cover up what is undesirable in their personal lives and character. As the leaves begin to fall—and they usually do—the exposure is painful.

When we go shopping, we realize that any disparity between what is shown in the window display and what is inside on the counter reveals the store's lack of integrity. So with personal character, the window dressings—if they are compensations—indicate trouble, not strength. The gap between the impressions one gives and the true inner condition signals trouble, regardless of the verdant covering on one's "tree."

Before we look further at the tools and guiding principles for helping troubled persons, let me relate a story that will illustrate the points covered thus far regarding responsibility and root issues. My wife and I were guests at dinner in the home of a young family with two children of grade-school age. I had been told of their difficulty with their young son. Now I saw it for myself. Meaningful conversation was all but impossible. No matter what Dad said, the boy did the opposite. When he was told to put away his toys and come to the table, he left his things where they were, scattered about the living room. The father meekly put away the toys.

Confusion reigned during the meal. Finally, the boy slipped under the dinner table and crawled about my wife's feet. In no uncertain terms, she ordered him up from there. The mother returned from the kitchen at that moment, and I noted that she was aggravated at my wife, not at her son.

Subsequently, the father visited my office and told me that the lad was being put on a drug therapy. Since it was so obvious that these parents failed to employ even the most basic principles of parenting, I wondered aloud to him, "Why is the boy the one who gets the drugs?"

I proposed a remedial approach to the whole troubled family, roughly in three phases. First I offered to help the man establish a more balanced relationship with his wife and to take up family leadership. Second, I pointed out their need of relationships with other, more wholesome families in the church so they could see firsthand how to employ parenting skills and how to build a loving marriage relationship. Third, I sought to help him envision what it would be like if his son and daughter were surrounded with consistent, loving discipline.

Later, as he and his wife talked over my proposals, they opted for what seemed to them to be the simplest solution—medicate the boy. In this particular case, it appeared to me that the parents were giving attention to painful symptoms and failing to address the roots of the difficulty.

## Bringing Relief to Troubled Persons

It is of critical importance to employ spiritual tools both for understanding and for relieving problems. In addition, any procedure of relief should be carried out in keeping with guiding principles given us in Scripture.

1. *Prayer.* A person struggles to make a bed in the dark but easily threads a needle in the light. Ask God for insight and wisdom as you counsel. In prayer, "turn on the light" by taking time to worship and glorify the Lord Jesus Christ. You can prepare your own heart for the counseling appointment by reading the final half of Ephesians 1. Then as you pray with your friend, ask that God's light shine deep into your hearts, making the real issues very clear. Remember, Jesus said, "I am the light of the world. Whoever follows me will never walk in darkness, but will have the light of life" (John 8:12).

2. *The Word.* A strong confidence in God's Word is necessary for discipling and counseling in the Spirit. When you know what the troubling matter is, things are put in perspective, for both counselor and counselee, when Scripture is read that bears on the subject. Even in cases where you might not have any specific idea of the problem and perhaps the friend in need is thoroughly confused and unable to verbalize their real difficulty, God's Word can still help if it is used properly.

A proper use of the Word will demand more than simply reading a portion devotionally at the beginning or ending of your appointment. Instead, in an attitude of reverence, read aloud a text that has been carefully selected to bring the Spirit's light, insight, and guidance in the interview. As the meeting progresses and more illumination is obtained, other Scriptures will come to mind that relate more specifically to the needs presented.

Here are examples of texts that I use to engender confidence and light, to quiet emotions, to bring openness, and to restore thankfulness for our salvation in Christ.

> The unfolding of your words gives light;
> it gives understanding to the simple.
> (Ps. 119:130)

For the word of God is living and active. Sharper than any double-edged sword, it penetrates even to dividing soul and spirit, joints and marrow; it judges the thoughts and attitudes of the heart. Nothing in all creation is hidden from God's sight. Everything is uncovered and laid bare before the eyes of him to whom we must give account. (Heb. 4:12-13)

For he has rescued us from the dominion of darkness and brought us into the kingdom of the Son he loves, in whom we have redemption, the forgiveness of sins. (Col. 1:13-14)

For in Christ all the fullness of the Deity lives in bodily form, and you have been given fullness in Christ, who is the head over every power and authority. (Col. 2:9-10)

He did not need man's testimony about man, for he knew what was in a man. (John 2:25)

Everyone who does evil hates the light, and will not come into the light for fear that his deeds will be exposed. But whoever lives by the truth comes into the light, so that it may be seen plainly that what he has done has been done through God. (John 3:20-21)

3. *Questions.* Generally, counsel is only as good as the

questions that precede it. Troubled persons either will not, or simply cannot, tell what their real problem is unless they are assisted by questions. One's self-monitoring mechanisms seem to break down under stress. At any rate, "The words of a man's mouth are deep waters" (Prov. 18:4), so questions are absolutely essential, for they bring disclosure for the counselor's benefit and also guide the counselee into self-understanding and willingness to cooperate.

It is imperative that those who disciple and counsel others learn to listen and observe—not only to what is said, but to how it is said. As people respond to each inquiry, attitudes and emotions surface and fill out the picture, "for out of the overflow of the heart the mouth speaks" (Matt. 12:34).

# 11

# TRUTH THAT
# BRINGS FREEDOM

"Then you will know the truth, and the truth will set you free." These words of Jesus, from John 8:32, are often quoted but not always put into practice in counseling. It would be sadly contradictory for a counselor to subscribe to the major truths of our faith and yet fail to counsel in their light.

Take time right now to reflect on the following list of major doctrines, considering how each truth might help troubled persons:

- God as Creator and mankind as his creation (For example: since the loving God is our Maker, he will know how to fix anything "broken" in what he's made, and he will have a compelling interest in resolving anything that troubles his creature.)
- the universality of sin and the resulting depravity of human nature
- Jesus Christ coming in human nature, his atonement for our sin, and his resurrection—all holding promise for us today
- our Lord's present occupation in heaven, opening the great door of prayer to each believer

- all the ministries of the Holy Spirit to us and within us
- the hope of Christ's return and our eternal home with him.

If you and I truly believe these momentous truths, we will turn to them in our own hour of need and keep them uppermost in our minds as we seek to edify others. Remember, my aim here is not to produce a treatise on counseling but to show the relationship between the help we give others and the truths we hold with clarity. When major truths are allowed to slide into the shadows and Christ distances himself from us, attempts at discipleship counseling will not have divine dynamic. In such cases, scaffolding of ongoing counseling might support a drooping person, and medicinal therapies might jump-start and assist in steadying the gait of a sufferer. But long-term negative results might still follow.

Let me give examples that illustrate the serious effects accompanying counseling procedures that omit a strong vertical alignment. As I bring these pictures before you, please notice carefully how, in each case, defective understanding of truth leaves the persons stranded and unprotected from the consequences that rain down upon them. Basic truths, as listed at the outset of this chapter and as expounded more fully in part 1, might well have spared them much suffering.

## "Ben Is Having a Breakdown Right Here and Now!"

Ben was desperate. He instinctively drove to the home of his friends Tom and Mary. Mary was shocked at his appearance and even more disturbed at his words. "Drinking has finally caught up to me. I'm ruined . . . nothing to live for . . . lost my job. Sonya has packed up and left with the kids. I can't handle things any more . . . falling to pieces!"

Seeing him trembling and hinting of taking his life sent Mary in a panic to the Yellow Pages in search of a church that might help. Though she was Catholic, out of deference to her Southern Protestant friend, she looked for one of his kind. That is how she happened to dial my church.

"Are you the 'father' of the church?" she blurted out. "Our friend Ben here is falling apart. Drinking and living it up has ruined him and his home. I'm afraid he's having a breakdown right here and now! Can you help?"

Ben managed to drive his sports car to the church office, and in walked what was once a handsome thirty-five-year-old man of the world. Now he was too distraught even to relate his story. Seeing he was so near the edge, I decided on an emergency approach.

"Ben, do you believe in the Lord Jesus Christ?" His answer was delivered in short, painful gasps of speech: "Yes, I'm saved . . . at my home church in Texas. I know about the Holy Ghost, too . . . but now I need help!" His words ended in a pleading wail. With eyes closed and head lowered, a trembling hand signaled that he could talk no further. He was sinking, and there was not a moment to lose.

I felt I must somehow arouse him to take hold of truth, but I had two difficult questions to face: What truth should I use? and How might I possibly get it over to him? What would you do to help this struggling, fainting man?

Breathing a short prayer, I jolted him with a question, causing his eyes to open and his head to lift. "Ben, here is a question maybe you haven't heard before: Where was Jesus before he was conceived in his mother's womb? (Please, keep your head up for a moment!) I didn't exist before my mother conceived me, nor did you. Was it any different with Jesus?"

Grimacing, he groaned out this response. "I don't know . . . never even thought of that. I reckon not."

Now I had discovered a truth he was missing and sorely needed. Just as I had sensed from the outset, his earlier spiritual experience had seemed real to him, but it was no match for the temptations that had dragged him into his present state.

With a burst of genuine excitement, I spoke more loudly, "There's your problem, Ben! Maybe now I can help. You've got the wrong Jesus!" As his eyes met mine with a questioning examination, I added quietly, "That Jesus you described does not exist."

Now he was bolt upright. With eyes wide open, he stammered, "What . . . what do you mean?"

Into that gaping heart, I poured in truth, in simple and brief sentences, explaining that the One who was eternal God stooped to the door of the womb to enter our world. I referred to John 1:14: the Son "became flesh and made his dwelling among us. We have seen his glory, the glory of the One and Only, who came from the Father, full of grace and truth."

"Ben, God himself came in human form and suffered on the cross for the very sin that is destroying you. But Jesus did not stay dead. He is now alive to hear and help you—right now." In a moment we were kneeling at our chairs there in my study. His prayer was earnest, honest, and offered with mounting hope.

Before I give the remarkable conclusion to our story, let me interject a defense for my "unprofessional" procedure. I am well aware of the standard rules for counseling that I appeared to break on that afternoon years back. I sensed at once, however, that Ben thought of himself as a believer in Christ and as one who held the Bible's teachings. To me, though, he looked rather like a woodsman inching his way out on an unsound limb. The further he went, the more certain his fall was becoming.

The limb of truth on which many begin their climb in life may not be very strong and sound. It is important, therefore, that we all gain more solid doctrinal support as we get on in our spiritual lives. Misconceptions regarding major truths will not support the weight of life's heavier trials. That was Ben's jeopardy. Attempting to relieve his troubled mind would not be enough. He was dangling over disaster from a belief system that was inadequate and cracking under the weight of his problems. I went there first, knowing that a spiritual renewal would make it easier to get him through to God's help. Here is what happened.

As we arose from our prayer, Ben was no longer agitated and shaking. His eyes were wide open, and he was able to converse with me more normally. "When did you last eat?" I asked. As I suspected, he had not been eating properly, so I phoned ahead to Jane to say that I was bringing a new friend home to dinner. Once we were in our home, my good wife, sensing the situation, put him entirely at ease and drew a smile from him.

As the meal progressed, Ben's transformation continued. Now he was relishing the opportunity to talk about his wife, Sonya, and the children. With mounting hope, he mused, "If only I could get her to come and talk with you."

The next morning the stylish, attractive young mother and wife sat in my office. Already she was convinced that some significant change had come into Ben's life, and she wanted to know what this was. Early in our interview, she admitted her own personal need to find peace with God and readily accepted the invitation to repent and turn in faith to Jesus Christ. Later that very day the family was reunited and returned to their home.

Seeing the strength of their new commitment to the Lord

and to one another, I gave them a special challenge. "Apparently your home is a gathering place for a number of couples who are special friends. Why not gather them for a different kind of 'party'? Tell them what new things Christ has done for you, and then begin a weekly Bible study."

With enthusiasm the invitation went out to a number of couples, who filled their living room to hear Ben and Sonya's story and to hear one of the men from our church teach them gospel truth. In time, nearly all of them became committed believers, including Mary, the friend who had originally phoned about Ben's need.

## A Hidden Root

Perhaps I should mention that Mary's decision to follow Christ had its own difficulties. She was radiant in giving testimony to her new faith—too radiant, I felt. It would have been very natural to give the emotional empathy and support she easily drew from all around her. I suspected, however, that the instability that marred her life (and worried her husband, who was not a believer) had a deeper root.

To many who counsel, the doctrine of sin is odious, especially if confronting a tearful, attractive client. More popular therapies, which have no real place for sin, would have left Mary's problem untouched. Eventually the deep root came to light. She had, in her past, been heavily involved with the occult, even leading séances. After a severe struggle, she renounced witchcraft and became a more stable Christian woman. Later, her husband joined her in the faith.

Turn again to figure 2 and notice occult practices as one of the limbs of sinful expression that might characterize a person privately, without it being commonly known. Such a practice, in turn, feeds back into the root system marked "chosen evil," thus completing a cycle of bondage. Sin tightens its grip as the practice continues.

On another occasion, when I sought to help a distraught professional man, he resisted any notion that he should repent of his sins against God. He had been encouraged to make the appointment with me by relatives in our church who were concerned about his talking of suicide. I pointed out to him that he seemed more willing to consider suicide than to consider repenting—to consider the grave rather than the arms of a loving Savior. This comment got us to a place where he was more ready to hear the truth of Scripture.

Jesus said to one whom he had healed, "See, you are well again. Stop sinning or something worse may happen to you" (John 5:14). Therefore we have it directly from our Lord: sin must not be overlooked, whether in the life of the sick or in the life of the well.

## A Common Confusion That Brings Disaster

Failing to distinguish clearly between God's provisions in Christ and his orders to us binds earnest souls in cycles of bitter defeat. Scripture *informs us of provisions*, but it *commands us regarding obligations*. For example, notice once again that these words from Colossians 3:3 do not order us to do anything, but they simply inform us of what has been accomplished by Christ: "For you died, and your life is now hidden with Christ in God."

The command "put to death, therefore, whatever belongs to your earthly nature" follows in the fifth verse. This passage shows the divine order in the working out of our salvation. First, we are told that we died with Christ when he died. Second, we are obligated to put to death sinful inclinations. The important essential to this personal release from guilt and sinful practice is to claim by faith the first (v. 3) and to rely on the Holy Spirit's help for our obedience to the second (v. 5). In other words, we must always base our obligations on God's provisions. What Christ has done in our place, he will work in our lives by the Holy Spirit, as we submit in obedience to him.

### "But I Can't Help It!"
Addictive behavior comes in many forms: chemical, sexual, and even habituated attitudes or actions—any one of which might be supported by an enabling relative, friend, or counselor.

Walter and I were chatting in my living room while Jane completed dinner preparations. I had moved beside him on the couch to point out helpful Bible verses. With obvious discomfort, he divulged his years of bondage to a habit. "You couldn't possibly understand what it's like. How often I have tried to quit, only to fall again! Every day I am exposed to the temptation. Over and over I try to resist, but I can't. It is hopeless!"

I shared with Walter a diagram of truth (see fig. 3), followed by the necessary instructions. The key verse for the diagram is Romans 6:14: "For sin shall not be your master, because you are not under law, but under grace." Notice the two arrangements (law or grace) under which we might live, and under which we might attempt to break a habit pattern. If a man is under the law, what are his resources? The law's regulations might tell us what is right and wrong, but we are not given help to do the right. Attempting on our own to regulate our behavior and break addictions inevitably ends with the cry that Walter sounded, "I can't!"

**Gracious Help**

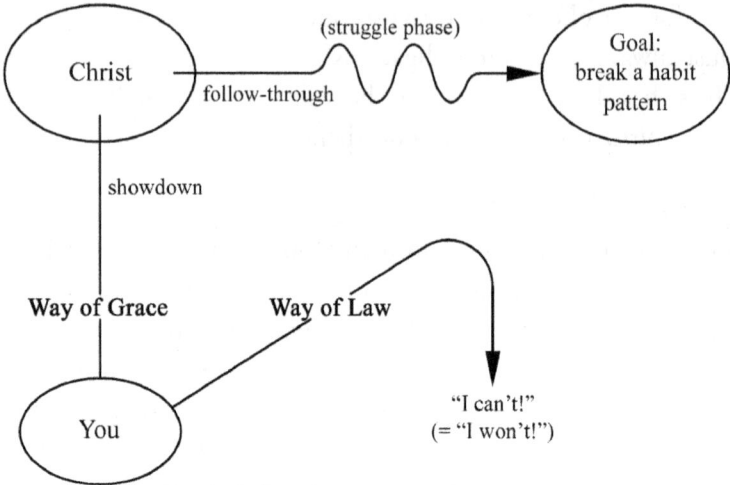

"For sin shall not be your master, because you are
not under law, but under grace." (Rom. 6:14)

Figure 3

Here is the truth Walter was missing: God, in grace, opens another way to us. See in the diagram how the way of grace is accompanied by a sufficient means to arrive at the goal. The Lord Jesus Christ is the means. His death on the cross pays the penalty of our sin, and his new life, lived in us by the Spirit, moves us to the longed-for victory. Then we can honestly say, "I can do *everything* through him who gives me strength" (Phil. 4:13).

Consider how truly gracious this arrangement is. In the effort to achieve the longed-for goal of freedom, we are not simply ordered to quit the sin. Turning away from an entrenched habit will likely seem impossible to the addicted one. Therefore let the counsel stress the provisions of grace—what our Lord did when he suffered on our behalf. This situation calls for repentance for the sin of abusing body and mind and a humble acceptance of

168

Christ's blood in payment for the sin. After this truth is made clear and definite and a true repentance has been made, the plea should be made to our Lord for help to live right, while relying on Scriptures like the text in figure 3, along with Philippians 4:13 and Romans 8:13 ("For if you live according to the sinful nature, you will die; but if by the Spirit you put to death the misdeeds of the body, you will live").

The first step in the way of grace is properly labeled on the diagram "showdown," for it involves repentance for the repeated sinful actions. Next, this surrender to the Lord Jesus leads one to acknowledge helplessness in breaking free of the sinful pattern, apart from the Spirit's gracious intervention. Exactly here, then, is the twofold nature of God's wondrous grace in dealing with fallen mortals: (1) Christ's gracious payment for the very sin that grips us, bringing forgiveness and right standing with God, and (2) divine enablement to live in freedom from the sinful practice, through the Spirit's special filling. In the light of such comprehensive grace, I insisted that Walter could never again say, "I can't." He must correct it to, "I won't!" This comment stunned him, and he made no attempt at rebuttal. It took a while for Walter to get free, but support from family and church and much prayer brought him into the light of a new life with God.

Problems in the horizontal dimension of life, so to speak, are what usually bring troubled persons to seek counsel. More often than not, however, the solutions require a vertical, spiritual realignment. Then God's intervention may be expected.

Since God's grace operates in this way in helping us sinners to freedom, we are without excuse if we continue in a sinful bondage. God not only provides for our forgiveness, he also offers gracious assistance to help us live a life of new freedom. We may not sit in our corner of rebellion and claim inability to escape the shadows. Further insights, however, will be required.

## Origin of a Problem

Making things right with our God means that we assume accountability to him in two regards: (1) the origin of our problem, and (2) the continuance of our problem. In this section we distinguish and explore these two points.

Examine again the root systems of the troubled personality diagram (fig. 2). It is easily seen that we are answerable for evils we have chosen to indulge in, but many resist the idea of accountability for the other roots. Think first about the left root. Indulging in sinful practices will mean a developing system of limbs above ground, though perhaps shaded from view by the leaves. These desires, if fed, have a determining effect on the life, bringing unwanted disorders. The animal keeper whose job it is to drop food for a young wild animal should in time expect to deal with a grown beast.

Check the limbs on the tree, left to right, as I describe what each indulgence might look like:

1. addiction to forms of immorality
2. occult experimentation and practice, superstitions
3. unforgiving spirit, hatred and resentment, refusal to make restitution
4. bondage to physical appetites
5. greed and materialistic pride, a drive for image, slavery to money and possessions.

Where any of these listed conditions prevail in a life, it is normal to show abnormalities in personality or practice. In the presence of sinful indulgence, it is counterproductive for a counselor or Christian friend to make the one in need comfortable enough to persist in wrong living.

No one can plead inability before an overpowering, destructive force in one's personal life without first examining the root causes for the problem. Repentance, then, means full admission for one's own contributions to the origin of the difficulty.

I must not only confess to God that I have chosen and committed this or that particular sin, but I must humbly admit that I *am* a sinner. This brings us to the two remaining root systems in our diagram. Responsibility must also be assumed for these roots. As explained in part 1 of this book, our inner corruptness of character is the initial death stroke of God's judgment against mankind's sin with, or through, Adam. Only salvation by faith in Jesus can remedy this powerful, central taproot of guilt. Once justified by Christ's blood, we then have access to the gracious help of God's Spirit and are no longer obliged to follow our sinful tendencies.

## Continuance of a Problem

Let's turn now to the third root. What about evils imposed on us by others in our personal environment? What if one's severe struggles with immorality are traceable to a deep infusion by childhood abuse of troubled, sinful desires into the depths of one's being? Or maybe there is a provable genetic inclination toward a particular sinful pattern. Is one still responsible in such cases?

First, when I approach God for his forgiveness and peace, I must own what I *am,* regardless of how that came about. Although—and this is important!—I cannot repent for sins done against me, I must frankly admit what I am, the sins I myself have chosen, and my need for the cleansing and strength of divine grace. True repentance in coming to the Father for grace doesn't include making excuses because of extenuating circumstances.

Now let's go a step further. Once a wrong practice in attitude or action has become a "part of us" and is habituated, our natural desires readily agree with the counsel often given that the blame is not ours. It feels better to blame environment or sinful persons who may have abused us and thus originated the troubling problem. But wait a moment—God's grace makes us accountable!

All our guilt is settled with God on the basis of the grace of our Lord Jesus Christ, whose blood is an offering for our sin. Thus, having right standing with God, you and I are free—not only from damnation—but free to appeal to God as our Father, begging him to extricate us from sin's stranglehold. Regardless of root causes, we may not continue what appears to be our "lot in life" if it is sinful. Whenever God requires change, his grace makes it possible. Christian counsel should clarify this point and assist those who are broken to take a confident hold on the full grace of God as taught in the Scriptures.

Even if in certain cases it can be proved that one is not responsible for becoming unable, one is surely accountable for remaining that way. Here again is that solemn truth: *grace makes us accountable.* Grace, then, works in this manner: First, my full repentance is met with gracious forgiveness from God. He forgives me for what I am as a sinner, and he wants to forgive me for the sinful practice that is disturbing my life. Second, as a reconciled Father, he is willing to put his arm around me and give spiritual strength to break free from sin's bondage. Continuing in sin reveals more than yielding to the pull of the temptation; it means refusing God's help and resisting his Spirit, as figure 3 shows. That refusal, as we have said, amounts to saying "I won't!" to God. This willful refusal, however, must be clearly distinguished from the up-and-down cycles of struggles that one might face on the way to the goal of release through Christ from sinful bondage, as the top, horizontal leg of figure 3 depicts.

It is therefore unnecessary for those chained in sinful habits to get to the place where they no longer crave the sin before they quit it. They must choose to turn to God in repentance and plead for Christ's personal help. A homely illustration might help. Suppose a young woman who is utterly addicted to chocolate candy receives a sinister gift of poisoned chocolates. The contents are beautiful, but an attached note warns, "Every piece of candy in this box is laced with arsenic!" The poor recipient is salivating profusely, but she does not have to get to the place where she no longer likes chocolate before she refuses the candy and is safe. Turning to Christ is more than a safe alternative; it is an alternative that is power-filled, for living a new life.

Now spend a few moments considering this question: If one is responsible for both the origin and the continuance of one's problem, is any true solution possible until blame is accepted?

## Taking Sin Seriously

Before concluding this counseling and discipling theme, two remaining major questions need answering. First, how much should sin figure into counseling? Second, how much should Satan figure into counseling? Must modern Christian counseling take sin and Satan seriously?

Choosing a doctrinal statement that includes a technically correct view of sin is commendable, but it does not guarantee a very serious concern and care about the whole matter of human sin. To substantiate my concern about the omission of sin in today's thought, look at the shelves of most Christian bookstores. Notice the large number of works that focus on me and my hurts and needs. The outcry "Why?" directed to, or even against, God is generally dignified with unquestioned approval. I am not here debating whether "Why me, Lord?" is ever appropriate. My concern is about the unspoken, underlying motivation—the feeling, "I deserve better than this!"

We have lost sight of the very ancient and now little-mentioned doctrine of human depravity. Adam's first sin and its impact on his entire lineage must be the point of reference as we evaluate and interpret God's dealings with those we counsel. Because this truth is so important to our subject of counseling, let's review it briefly. We all are born guilty! This judgment was passed at once on Adam and all his line. He is our father, and we bear his name and legal status. When Adam sinned, it is credited to all who are born into his lineage. It is impossible, under God's just rule, for guilt not to be punished, hence God warned Adam ahead of time, "When you [sin], you will surely die" (Gen. 2:17). Adam did sin, and this sin is also *our* sin, for we are his children. The death sentence that came on Adam and all his line includes inner depravity and ultimately physical death as well.

The Judge thus declares us guilty, and we labor under the bondage and brokenness of our sinful condition. He nevertheless calls us to see that he "demonstrates his own love for us in this: While we were still sinners, Christ died for us. Since we have now been justified by his blood, how much more shall we be saved from God's wrath through him! For if, when we were God's enemies, we were reconciled to him through the death of his Son, how much more, having been reconciled, shall we be saved through his life!" (Rom. 5:8-10).

The problem of sin necessarily figures into counseling, edification, and discipling in the Christian community for two very outstanding reasons. First, look at the death of Christ on the cross. Sin is so serious as to require the death of Christ and all the great provisions of salvation, including the ongoing work of the Holy Spirit. Next, look at every person who is being discipled or counseled. Every one, without exception, is a sinner. This universal plague cannot be ignored in the name of love or in the name of psychology.

Let me prove my point. Suppose a certain counselor's book of appointments lists clientele whose difficulties include the following assortment of complaints:

1. I keep hoping for a break, but everything is so dark! I'm creeping through life as if blind. My heart groans and growls, and I see no way out!
2. I am failing physically; my strength is gone. God is squashing me!
3. My health has failed because inwardly I am so troubled and burdened. I am overwhelmed!
4. I simply cannot get through to God. Is there no comfort for me?
5. I thought God was a God of grace. Look what's happening to me!

If you were their counselor, what tack would you take with these people and their problems? What do you think might be the approach of a typical counselor?

Such cases make a very important point. I have drawn each of these five signals of distress directly from Scripture. But there is more. The texts make it clear in each case that the pain of the ones who suffer is a result of their own sin. Please verify this connection by reviewing the following texts, in which sin is confessed as the cause of the complaints:

1. For our offenses are many in your sight, and our sins testify against us. Our offenses are ever with us, and

we acknowledge our iniquities. (Isa 59:12; notice the complaints in vv. 9-11)

2. Then I acknowledged my sin to you and did not cover up my iniquity. I said, "I will confess my transgressions to the Lord"—and you forgave the guilt of my sin. (Ps. 32:5; notice the complaints in vv. 3-4)

3. Because of your wrath there is no health in my body; my bones have no soundness because of my sin. My guilt has overwhelmed me like a burden too heavy to bear. . . . I confess my iniquity; I am troubled by my sin. (Ps. 38:3-4, 18)

4. Their deeds do not permit them to return to their God. A spirit of prostitution is in their heart; they do not acknowledge the Lord. . . . When they go . . . to seek the Lord, they will not find him; he has withdrawn himself from them. . . . Then I will go back to my place until they admit their guilt. And they will seek my face; in their misery they will earnestly seek me. (Hos. 5:4, 6, 15)

5. Those who cling to worthless idols forfeit the grace that could be theirs. (Jonah 2:8)

The question is now before us: May we assume, without question, that pitiable cries of suffering are *not* traceable to sin and a distancing from God? No, sin is a reality in all lives and must be recognized as the possible root or at least the exacerbation of critical issues requiring counseling. Even if, as in figure 2, people are dealing with an "imposed evil," they still need to approach the Father with faith in his grace to fully deal with even this kind of need. Otherwise, they too might find out that "the way of the unfaithful is hard" (Prov. 13:15), exactly as the five texts above make clear. Imagine the futility of counseling aimed at bringing peace into the lives of those who are holding on to sin and avoiding repentance! "There is no peace," the Lord says, "for the wicked" (Isa. 48:22).

Tears in the eyes of the needy should not disarm the one who would assist. It must be held steadily in mind that sin must be evaluated by its offence to God, not by how it seems to us. Long ago two men wept bitter tears on the same night. If you had encountered them, how would you have proceeded in helping? Would you have been more concerned about helping them to peace or about helping them to repentance? Their names: Peter and Judas. Both were deeply troubled and sorrowful, but only Peter moved on to repentance. Such a difference in grieving and in the two responses is well summarized in 2 Corinthians 7:10: "Godly sorrow brings repentance that leads to salvation and leaves no regret, but worldly sorrow brings death."

I have included a letter in appendix 7 that addresses the burden of explaining sin and death to a young child. I wrote to parents who were facing hard questions from their very bright and sensitive daughter of about seven years old after her mother's miscarriage had shattered her hope of being a big sister to the new baby.

As suggested earlier, Satan must be reckoned with as we take up a discipling and counseling ministry. I treat this subject separately, in chapter 12.

## Concluding Observations

Counseling as if the root systems of sin distinguished in figure 2 do not exist is unthinkable. Just as it matters what cruel pressures have figured into a life, so it also matters what choices one has made. Even binding habits are born and nurtured initially by choice. Furthermore, when the main taproot of guilt is ignored,

God and his judgment of human sin are essentially denied. In such cases, solutions will be elusive, incomplete, and short-lived, since only the painful symptoms are being dealt with. Real causes are left untouched.

Nothing leaks air as fast as a self-image inflated by counsel that does not come to grips with real causes. Such unfortunate ones will require much anxious attention and continual pumping. A man who does not think well of himself may think most often about himself. Such faulty self-appraisal is often fortified with the vain, uncritical view of God as always forgiving, no matter what. Even a casual review of those who have received this treatment will show that they have learned only to drag their bonds more gracefully.

Expecting the blessings of grace to be automatic and to supersede all our volition is sheer presumption. God requires his child to be diligent in appropriating all his gracious provisions. Passivity, a suffocating quagmire, is often but a covering for rebellion against God and all that is right. This rebellion becomes evident when the offer of God's grace is refused. "I can't" and "I won't" are vastly different. God's grace meets the need of human inability as long as it is not resisted. "His divine power has given us everything we need for life and godliness through our knowledge of him who called us by his own glory and goodness" (2 Peter 1:3). A fellow believer can make this truth clear and useful to one in need.

"See to it, brothers, that none of you has a sinful, unbelieving heart that turns away from the living God. But encourage one another daily, as long as it is called Today, so that none of you may be hardened by sin's deceitfulness" (Heb. 3:12-13). The condition of the members of God's family is the responsibility of fellow believers. Sin's deceitfulness presses us all, if allowed, into a spiritual hardness and a turning away from the God we sorely need. The way wounded and faltering sheep are so often tended today places the responsibility for their recovery and healing on resources outside the church. (I discuss God's arrangement for accomplishing this ministry *within* the local church in chapter 13.)

As we finish our study of discipleship counseling, let me bring into sharper focus our purpose for this discussion. I have not undertaken to write on how to counsel. Rather, my aim has been to show how serious and fundamental is the departure when counseling silences God's call to repentance and allows major truths of the Christian faith to slip from view.

With little or no spiritual inventory or serious inquiry into a counselee's spiritual life, the clinician is appealed to, and the church lays aside its tools given by the Spirit for the care of God's flock. But what if the wounded one is beloved of God in the sense of Hebrews 12, where we are taught about painful discipline (see v. 11) being a significant expression of our Father's great love? "And you have forgotten that word of encouragement that addresses you as sons: 'My son, do not make light of the Lord's discipline, and do not lose heart when he rebukes you, because the Lord disciplines those he loves, and he punishes everyone he accepts as a son'" (vv. 5-6). Are not some counselors guilty of trying to hold back the hand of a loving Father who shows love by disciplining his child?

Or at the other end of the spectrum, what if a broken, troubled person should be one of those who "became fools through their rebellious ways and suffered affliction because of their iniquities" (Ps. 107:17)? Such people will naturally spurn the help of the church and seek a pill that goes down easier, for "fools mock at making amends for sin" (Prov. 14:9). Furthermore, "a man who strays from the path of understanding comes to rest in the company of the dead" (Prov. 21:15). It is of the nature of spiritual decline to continue until spiritual means of release and rescue are employed. It is not unkind to seek out and ameliorate the real cause in cases like those mentioned in the Scriptures.

I have sought to show that an emphasis on love and grace must not lead us to overlook those persons who have unnoticed problem areas of sin. Balance must be maintained so that a proper emphasis on love and grace will not incline toward a presumptuous looseness in living. Those who taste the sweetness of God's forgiveness will love and revere him in return. "But with you there is forgiveness; therefore you are feared" (Ps. 130:4).

# 12

# THE INVISIBLE WAR

Our spiritual war may be called invisible from two points of view. In the first place, our great enemy Satan is an invisible, spiritual entity. Second, his operations in our visible realm are often done with incredible deceptions. Shots that are silent and unseen are all the more deadly.

"Spiritual warfare" is a popular subject in certain quarters today, but the colossal struggle spoken about in Scripture is never popular. Furthermore, apart from the grand truths covered in part 1, the Christian combatant is only shadowboxing, without footing or adequate foundation to resist—let alone conquer—our mighty foe the devil.

## Superhuman Power

Satan is too much for us to handle, and Scripture warns, "Woe to the earth and the sea, because the devil has gone down to you! He is filled with fury, because he knows that his time is short" (Rev. 12:12). According to the Bible, he has now ensconced himself as "the prince of this world" (John 12:31), "the god of this age" (2 Cor. 4:4), and "the ruler of the kingdom of the air" (Eph. 2:2). "The whole world is under the control of the evil one" (1 John 5:19); he "leads the whole world astray" (Rev. 12:9).

The appearing of Jesus is linked in Matthew 2:5-6 to the

prophet Micah's prediction of the future "ruler who will be the shepherd of my people Israel." But Satan counters the Good Shepherd's coming by his own "coming." Jesus taught: "The thief comes only to steal and kill and destroy; I have come that they may have life, and have it to the full" (John 10:10). So it is that "our struggle is not against flesh and blood, but against the powers of this dark world and against the spiritual forces of evil in the heavenly realms" (Eph. 6:12).

In the light of this dark truth, it will be seen that drawing people out of the devil's grasp and influence will require special help from God. This divine assistance is available as we by faith align ourselves with Jesus Christ and receive the Holy Spirit, who comes to live in us. And "the one who is in you is greater than the one who is in the world" (1 John 4:4).

## The Only Way to Fight

Two opposite extremes regarding Satan must be avoided: to be always looking him over or to be always overlooking him. Our focus must be on Jesus Christ, but we must not forget our enemy. Given Satan's superhuman power, we must choose wisely the ground on which we make our stand. We dare not pit our might against his. Instead, we stand on our *right* against his *might*. Our condemnation and terrible deficit position before God are changed by the sacrifice of Christ on our behalf. By the cross, the devil is overthrown in the sense of losing his rights over the children of God: "And having disarmed the powers and authorities, he made a public spectacle of them, triumphing over them by the cross" (Col. 2:15). Our enemy has the might— enough to enslave and ruin us—but he does not have the right to do it as we stand our ground in Jesus' name.

Our privilege of living free from demonic influence and then assisting others to step into this liberty comes down to the matter of setting authority above strength. This distinction need not be an opaque riddle, for comments by Jesus in Luke 10 imply just this contrast. In verse 3 he highlights our very limited and totally inadequate strength: "I am sending you out like lambs among wolves." But then in verse 19 he makes clear the vast scope of the authority he gives us: "I have given you *authority* to trample on snakes and scorpions and to overcome *all the power* of the enemy; nothing will harm you." Therefore, as we sense our weakness before Satan's immense power, we are driven to rely solely on the position of authority given us by our Lord. The authority of the frail judge prevails over the muscle of the strong criminal—but let not the magistrate be provoked into a hand-to-hand contest! Our strength is in the Lord. Our spiritual weapons are designed to employ his power against that of the enemy. In the name of the Lord we have the right, the authority, to do exactly that.

## The Devil's Procedure

The Bible reveals Satan's tactics. Our being aware of his schemes can prevent him from taking advantage of us (see 2 Cor. 2:11 and Eph. 6:11). These procedures may be stated simply, but they are in fact complex and varied. I discuss here three of the devil's major devices: deception, seduction, and accusation. By the first two, Satan arranges for our falls; by the third, he attempts to keep us down.

## Deception

A Christian can be deceived and lose perspective of right and wrong in one of two ways: by a shutdown of light or by blindness.

We are counseled in God's Word to walk in the truth and live by the Word. This dedication to Scripture requires our daily attention to it and enables us to walk with Christ and to live "in the Spirit." If this attention to Scripture is neglected and our life of prayer and fellowship wanes, light dims. Just as it is impossible for darkness to overcome light, so it is impossible to keep out shadows when light dims.

Dullness in spiritual perception and carelessness in behavior very often steal in unannounced. Through this means, the Deceiver sets up his prey for the takedown. No warning trumpets signal to us that sinful practices, being repeated, lead into addiction and the inclination to even more serious evils.

> The god of this age has blinded the minds of unbelievers, so that they cannot see the light of the gospel of the glory of Christ, who is the image of God. (2 Cor. 4:4)

> For you were once darkness, but now you are light in the Lord. Live as children of light (for the fruit of the light consists in all goodness, righteousness and truth) and find out what pleases the Lord. Have nothing to do with the fruitless deeds of darkness, but rather expose them. For it is shameful even to mention what the disobedient do in secret. But everything exposed by the light becomes visible, for it is light that makes everything visible. This is why it is said: "Wake up, O sleeper, rise from the dead, and Christ will shine on you." (Eph. 5:8-14)

## Seduction

Satan's schemes aim at preventing God's child from exercising his or her will—not only in choosing moral right but in choosing to take hold of the means of God's grace. The latter choice, once it is made, will in turn enable one to make the former choice. Review this principle by returning to figure 3, "Gracious Help," in chapter 11.

Some demons purr and coo. (I mean this comment seriously

and not at all facetiously.) Things utterly devilish are made to appear delightful and winsome. The tempter entwines the will without the sound of jangling chains. Instead, natural desires are fed in such a way that the victim not only cooperates with the enemy but even resists freedom.

Once evil is chosen, subjection to sin, or habituation, follows. Notice the place of "chosen evil" in figure 2, "The Troubled Personality," in chapter 10. Satan never passes by an open door. A pattern of sinful practice enslaves the volition and gives the devil a measure of control. Refer to the limbs in figure 2 and consider again this list of sins, which, if practiced, will become the root of severe bondage:

1. immorality in mind or actions
2. occult experimentation
3. an unforgiving spirit, hate, resentment, refusal to make restitution
4. allowing appetites to rule
5. commitment to materialism, greed, pride, drive for prominence.

A moral collapse that observers may describe as a sudden fall might have been in the works for a long while. Satan will work patiently over years, or decades if necessary, to cause one grievous fall. The evidences of a developing disaster may not be noticed, but they are there. For example, believing a lie and living as if it were true leads to habituated practice of sin. Satan's allurements resonate with carnal desires, and when the will ceases to function against evil, it makes common cause with the enemy against God and right.

**Accusation**
The devil's piercing reminders of past sin rip the conscience and

keep it raw and bleeding. Bewailing our failures might weaken us, but it cannot strengthen us. The enemy's accusations, deep within, perpetuate the evil effects of a fall into sin and render the defeated one more likely to fall again.

Nothing except an enlightened use of the benefits of Christ's death can withstand the withering effects of evil-spirit accusation. This defense will be considered now in connection with an overall strategy for resisting and overcoming our great enemy.

## How to Wield God's Strength

One who is under Satan's assault must at the very outset move from discouraging darkness into the light of truth. This done, the devil loses much of his advantage. Remember, fight your battles in the light.

Here is how to turn on the light, or, putting it another way, to choose the ground on which you will fight. In specific, definite prayer, make a full-orbed confession of Jesus Christ as your Lord and Savior. (Whether you are the one who is troubled, or whether you are endeavoring to help a friend, the following words should prove beneficial.) See figure 4, which clarifies what is meant by a full-orbed confession.

It is insufficient merely to claim allegiance to a proper doctrinal statement. Our real confession is what we put front and center in our living and praying, and these vital truths need to be reiterated in a fresh way regularly. As figure 4 indicates, we wholeheartedly confess in a definite prayer that Jesus Christ has come to us in human form, as 1 John 4:2-3 states: "Every spirit that acknowledges that Jesus Christ has come in the flesh is from God, but every spirit that does not acknowledge Jesus is not from God. This is the spirit of the antichrist, which you have heard is coming and even now is already in the world."

**Full-Orbed Confession**

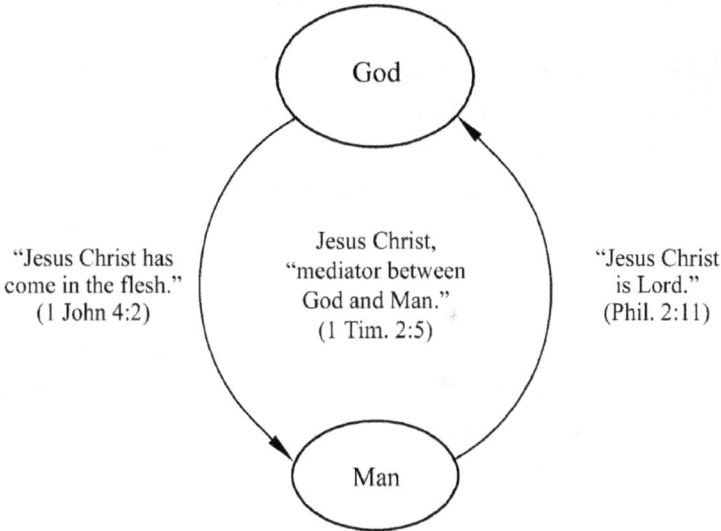

"Jesus Christ has come in the flesh." (1 John 4:2)

Jesus Christ, "mediator between God and Man." (1 Tim. 2:5)

"Jesus Christ is Lord." (Phil. 2:11)

God

Man

Figure 4

Our aim, then, is to align ourselves with the Holy Spirit's word that Christ is God incarnate, which can disassociate us from any evil presence. Notice next the strength of Philippians 2:9-11. The confession "Jesus Christ is Lord" positions our Savior over all other authorities and affirms our place under his rule. First Corinthians 12:3 might also be added here: "No one can say, 'Jesus is Lord,' except by the Holy Spirit." Making this strong affirmation in prayer—even audibly—will shut out Satan, as we stand in the light of this powerful truth.

Finally, I have often experienced release from stifling spiritual darkness, both in my personal contests and in my efforts to counsel others, by using an additional text that relates to the themes of figure 4. In prayer, every phrase of this Scripture should be affirmed strongly: "For in Christ all the fullness of the Deity lives in bodily form, and you have been given fullness in Christ, who is the head over every power and authority" (Col. 2:9-10).

## The Kind of Prayer That Brings Release and Freedom

Without exception, the adversary takes advantage over those who fail to resist him as God commands: "Submit yourselves, then, to God. Resist the devil, and he will flee from you" (James 4:7). "Be self-controlled and alert. Your enemy the devil prowls around like a roaring lion looking for someone to devour. Resist him, standing firm in the faith, because you know that your brothers throughout the world are undergoing the same kind of sufferings" (1 Peter 5:8-9). It is plainly stated here that combat with Satan is not an exceptional experience but is to be expected by all believers. What shall we say of those who attempt to live as if this were not the case? And what of those who counsel and train others to overlook this reality?

The critical showdown with the devil and his emissaries must be done in a definite prayer. A weak moaning will not do. The prayer should be strongly put. I have found it helpful to others to sketch in writing an outline of the prayer to be used. I employ the acronym "BLAST" to aid memory. Following are suggestions for the prayer, along with comments and Scriptures to support each portion.

*Blood*—Claim the blood of Jesus Christ as payment for the sin(s), mentioned by name.

>Being definite is important—both in pleading the blood before God and in specifically naming the sin or sins that have troubled one's relations with the Lord. Serious sin offers the devil ground on which to stand and to wield leverage over the life. You must

now take back this advantage. In making the plea, look away from the sins once you have named them in confession, and read aloud 1 John 1:7: "If we walk in the light, as he is in the light, we have fellowship with one another, and the blood of Jesus, his Son, purifies us from all sin."

*Lord*—Confess and announce that Jesus Christ is Lord over all, and particularly over your life.

This lordship is not to be assumed only. It must be declared, using Scriptures like Colossians 1:13-14: "He has rescued us from the dominion of darkness and brought us into the kingdom of the Son he loves, in whom we have redemption, the forgiveness of sins."

*Authority*—Jesus is Lord and therefore has all authority. Standing in the name and authority of the Lord Jesus Christ, I order Satan out of my life, or I assist my friend in doing so.

You don't dialogue with the devil, but you must turn from compromise and make a stand against him. This step is more than simply begging God to help. You may count on God to help, as he promises; therefore, in the name of the Lord Jesus Christ, you resist the enemy and order him out of your life. Looking toward the cross, Jesus said, "Now the prince of this world will be driven out" (John 12:31). Colossians 2:15 is also powerful here.

*Spirit*—Claim the filling of the Holy Spirit.

You are not creating a spiritual vacuum; instead, you must earnestly replace sin with new openness to the Spirit in your life, just as Ephesians 5:18 directs: "Do not get drunk on wine, which leads to debauchery. Instead, be filled with the Spirit."

*Thanks*—Offer heartfelt thanks to the Lord.

Without waiting to take stock of feelings, pour out your thanks to God for everything that comes to mind—spiritual benefits, family, church, material things, and the beauty and wonders of nature. Give no quarter to confusing doubts; fill the mind with gratitude to God: "It is good to praise the LORD" (Ps. 92:1).

## What's Next?

Those recently released from some spiritual bondage will not necessarily escape from conflict. Indeed, their new struggles will tend to mimic their old ones. But there is a difference—a very great difference. This distinction can be visualized by referring to figure 3, "Gracious Help," in chapter 11.

Notice the two possible outcomes in figure 3. A man following the way of law ends up in despair, crying, "I can't!" which is ultimately shown to be, "I won't!" In contrast, a man pursuing the way of grace arrives at the very goal his heart desires. Now look again at the contrasting ways that are traveled. The failing one is trying on his own to keep all the right rules and thus arrive at the goal. He is in no condition before God, or within his heart, to do so.

In contrast with the futility of that way, the other way heads in a direction that ultimately leads to success. Such a one first truly repents of his sin and lawbreaking. Thus submitting to Christ as Lord, he makes a personal claim on both forgiveness and gracious help for living.

One who goes through Jesus Christ in this manner is thus

launched toward a goal of personal freedom on the route labeled "follow-through." More spiritual warfare marks this phase of Christian experience. The Deceiver and Accuser sharpens his attacks with this accusation: "Things are no different! You have fallen back into the old way again." A little reflection will expose this trickery, for these temptations can be distinguished from the former state of bondage. That is, the inevitable ups and downs of a truly repentant one who is relying on God's mercy and grace are very different from the collapse of one who is relying on his or her own resources.

### A Further Use of the BLAST Prayer

An area of advantage allowed to Satan will not be given up easily by him. Furthermore, even after help is given, each critical breakthrough must be followed up with steadfast and aggressive praying until the new victory is secure. This warfare praying may be done effectively by taking the BLAST showdown prayer and using it now for ongoing warfare praying.

Instead of opening each prayer with repentance for troubling sin, however, you will be praising God for the blood of the Savior, which guarantees your forgiveness. Everything else in the prayer is the same, only you are using the strongly worded prayer to affirm your right to full release in the name of the Lord Jesus Christ. Every time you sense rising feelings of fearful doubts or of the old sinful desires, you must tirelessly meet them with a fresh announcement of faith, through your battle prayer. If you don't give up, Satan will. He will not continue to do that which draws such weapons against him.

### What about Demon Possession?

Can a Christian be demon-possessed? This question has brought much confusion, even division, into certain segments of the church. A large part of the misunderstanding might be avoided if terms of the debate were first defined. For example, when the word "possession" is used, it seems to connote "ownership." Many of those who speak of demon possession, however, do not hold that ownership of one who is so subjugated has changed from God to the devil.

Keep in mind that we are now speaking only of believers in Christ who have failed to follow God's warning to resist the devil, as given in James 4:7 and 1 Peter 5:9. What happens to those who toy with sin and do not stand against the adversary? Will the devil not take control of areas that are not defended against him? Should we be surprised that the devil enters each door of opportunity that swings open to him? Using this entry, he begins manipulating the life, to the full extent of whatever leverage he can establish.

Consider the sad but common case of one who, by continuing in some sin, has allowed the devil to control an area of life. It is a grave wrong to disobey our Lord and allow place and leverage to Satan. The devil has no right to dominate God's child, but our enemy will go as far as the believer allows. This defeated Christian may repeatedly plead for God's forgiveness, but if the ground given to evil spirits is not retaken in the name of the Lord, nothing will really change. It behooves each Christian to watch and pray and, when there has been signal failure, to employ the strong countermeasures summarized in the BLAST prayer.

The right kind of praying will involve the substantial truths that are set forth in part 1 and that underlie this second part. Those oppressed must be counseled to stand in Jesus' name against their foe, being "strong in the Lord and in his mighty power" (Eph. 6:10). As this passage of the Word shows us, "Our struggle is not against flesh and blood, but against the rulers, against the authorities, against the powers of this dark world and against the spiritual forces of evil in the heavenly realms" (v. 12). Such an encounter requires all the armor, especially the shield of faith and the brave use of "the sword of the Spirit, which is the word of God" (v. 17).

A number of Bible texts with specific truths about the person and work of the Savior also clearly set forth the defeat of Satan, for example, John 12:31, Hebrews 2:14-15, and Revelation 12:11. The atoning death of Christ, when claimed in definite prayer, utterly disarms the devil. His designs are disrupted and destroyed.

One who is facing temptation, deadly sickness, or other tormenting trials must see to it that no hindrance stands between him or her and God. Through the cross, God's justice is satisfied. All charges against the troubled one may be transferred to Jesus' account. His death pays all and assures a warm welcome by the Father. Then, "if God is for us, who can be against us?" (Rom. 8:31).

## Practical Principles for Fighting the Battle

- To be tempted severely is not to fall necessarily. Do not accept Satan's line that you must go down again.
- Do not expect to stand or to withstand if you do or allow that which stimulates and excites wrong desires. One cannot both practice sin and have sweet assurance of God's forgiveness.
- Sin, like bananas, comes in bunches. One banana should make us look for more. A pattern tends to be repeated, and one type of sin breeds other kinds of sin. Satan is ever ready to supervise this process.
- Harboring ill feelings toward others is a serious sin that opens the door to Satan. Love is inspired by the Holy Spirit. Hatred

is inspired by the devil, the murderer.

- The reason is clear why much preaching, teaching, counseling, and witnessing is powerless to set spiritual prisoners free: "In fact, no one can enter a strong man's house and carry off his possessions unless he *first ties up the strong man*. Then he can rob his house" (Mark 3:27). God's servant, speaking in Christ's name and praying in the Spirit, can bind the strong enemy and lead out the hapless captives.

- With God on our side, it is not necessary for us to be as strong as our adversary. See such texts as Psalm 18:17; 35:10; 142:6, and Jeremiah 31:11.

- The mere fervency of the heart's ejaculations does not determine the power of our confessions. Repeating, "Jesus, Jesus! Yes, Jesus!" is not so effective as confessing *which* Jesus—like this: "Jesus Christ, you have come to us in flesh, and you are the Lord over all."

- When parents fail to guard the door of their homes and families against evil spirits, they might themselves become a point of entry into their homes. So also pastors who fail to be alert and watchful to guard the door of their churches tend to become a door for mischief.

- Satan whispers "grace" in the ear of the tempted one and "law" in the ear of the fallen one. Misguided counselors make the messages audible.

- Our enemy medicates his followers so they can function for him without being aware of it—so that they can look forward to heaven while headed for hell. Those who live terribly and are awakened to it are better off than those who appear more acceptable while living for self, sin, and Satan and are asleep to the issue of judgment to come.

- The fatally wounded snake thrashes more wildly and is more fearsome than the silent, coiled serpent. Satan often howls and threatens most when he has been defeated and is being successfully pressed to quit a territory.

- There are seasons in the spiritual life. Jesus once said to his foes, "This is your hour—when darkness reigns" (Luke 22:53). "Let him who walks in the dark, who has no light, trust in the name of the Lord and rely on his God" (Isa. 50:10).
- When you are oppressed with intrusive, dark thoughts, always ask who is talking. Set before you specific promises of God, and decisively trust what God says.
- Praise breaks the back of the mood monster, so let "the praise of God be in their mouths and a double-edged sword in their hands." Still further, the saints who know God's Word are given authority against their foes "to carry out the sentence written against them" (Ps. 149:6, 9).

## Concluding Comments

There is no question that Satan must be reckoned with when we are trying to minister to others. Hear what even the apostle Paul says about the devil's opposition as he confides to the Thessalonians, "Out of our intense longing we made every effort to see you. For we wanted to come to you—certainly I, Paul, did, again and again—but Satan stopped us" (1 Thess. 2:17-18). Furthermore, Paul recognized the need to hold the ground gained in believers' lives: "I sent to find out about your faith. I was afraid that in some way the tempter might have tempted you and our efforts might have been useless" (3:5).

What of those who are yet without any new life in Christ? Consider this sobering Scripture:

> As for you, you were dead in your transgressions and sins,

195

> in which you used to live when you followed the ways of
> this world and of the ruler of the kingdom of the air, the
> spirit who is now at work in those who are disobedient.
> All of us also lived among them at one time, gratifying the
> cravings of our sinful nature and following its desires and
> thoughts. Like the rest, we were by nature objects of wrath.
> (Eph. 2:1-3)

Our situation would indeed be black, were it not for the
verses that follow:

> But because of his great love for us, God, who is rich in
> mercy, made us alive with Christ even when we were dead
> in transgressions—it is by grace you have been saved. And
> God raised us up with Christ and seated us with him in the
> heavenly realms in Christ Jesus, in order that in the coming
> ages he might show the incomparable riches of his grace,
> expressed in his kindness to us in Christ Jesus. (vv. 4-7)

The challenge of evangelism is to convey the good news of
verses 4-7 and rescue people from the bondage of verses 1-3.
Then the challenge of discipleship counseling is to help liberated
ones remain free and, in turn, help others. Elsewhere, Paul insists
that the Lord's servant, even if opposed, "must gently instruct, in
the hope that God will grant them repentance leading them to a
knowledge of the truth, and that they will come to their senses
and escape from the trap of the devil, who has taken them captive
to do his will" (2 Tim. 2:25-26).

The adversary of believers is little disturbed by many human
efforts to free people from his grasp if the risen Lord Jesus Christ
is not a vital part of the counseling therapy. I also doubt that
Satan cares much about manuals written to unseat him so long
as there is no revival of the serious truths that form the heart of
God's real kingdom.

Here are two final messages—the first to those who might have become a bit lax, and the second to the battle-weary:

> Rescue those being led away to death; hold back those staggering toward slaughter. If you say, "But we knew nothing about this," does not he who weighs the heart perceive it? Does not he who guards your life know it? Will he not repay each person according to what he has done? (Prov. 24:11-12)

> When the storm has swept by, the wicked are gone, but the righteous stand firm forever. (Prov. 10:25)

# 13

# THE CHURCH IN CHRIST

Jesus promised, "I will build my church, and the gates of Hades will not overcome it" (Matt. 16:18). By this statement he surely was not putting everything having to do with the church at our discretion. Far from it! He holds the church close to his heart. Scripture shows the church to be the bride of Christ, and he cares very much how she behaves and appears. The Word also tells us that believers are "members of God's household, built on the foundation of the apostles and prophets, with Christ Jesus himself as the chief cornerstone. In him the whole building is joined together and rises to become a holy temple in the Lord. And in him you too are being built together to become a dwelling in which God lives by his Spirit" (Eph. 2:19-22).

With Christ as its chief cornerstone, everything about the church must fit and fasten to him. The church's structure and functions are not matters of merely optional styles. How, then, are we to account for the extensive variety and differences seen in the expression of Christianity worldwide? On the one hand, we see the most austere, ornate formalism, with its colorful pageantry in awe-inspiring cathedrals, and on the other hand, the most ineloquent rantings of crusaders for the extremes. In societies where Christianity is more prominent, it exists in a maze of denominations. Churches on the same street are not the same in structure and function. Indeed, many of them proudly emphasize their distinctives.

To help us find our way through the maze, we consider the following points:

1. Basics of the church and its life
2. Using Scripture to distinguish between merely human ideas and divine imperatives
3. Using part 1 to measure the separation of churches from their Head
4. Examples from contemporary church life
5. What about house churches?
6. Concluding thoughts.

## 1. Basics of the Church and Its Life

All believers together form Christ's body, the new creation, and this new company is located and seen in the churches. Exactly what is a church? Answer: it is a local replica of *the* church universal. More than simply a part, each local church is a representation of the whole.

Each church has Christ as its Head. False notions abound at this point. Some deny the local church its authority under Christ's headship. Even where there is strong connection with other churches, as in a denomination, each local church should value its own integrity. Others fail to distinguish any meeting of two or three believers from a meeting of a church. Both these extremes are corrected in such passages as Matthew 18:15-20. Notice carefully here that the Lord's authority is vested in these believers' own church. Indeed, Christ honors the two or three believers who reach out to an erring brother in his name by standing with them. Let no one reason from this passage, however, that a local church is not to be distinguished from the two or three members of the church. Read again verse 17, where they are distinguished from their church. These on mission are part of their church, but not a church.

Contrary to published teachings that wherever believers meet, there is a church, Scripture shows us that an assembly is an authentic church only when it has the life and form that is biblical. Minimally, there must be an elder (ideally, more than one) and believers. The eldership must fulfill its commission to teach and train the believers, helping them recognize and utilize all their gifts.

Most churches meet weekly to worship God corporately. This function is essential. Two other functions are also assigned to a church and must be seen in every assembly if it is to have biblical authenticity. First, the church is to proclaim gospel truth; second, the church is to disciple and build up all who believe. These two functions underlie the church's development in the Book of Acts: "The church throughout Judea, Galilee and Samaria . . . was strengthened; and encouraged by the Holy Spirit, it grew in numbers, living in the fear of the Lord" (9:31). We see the same functions in 16:5: "So the churches were strengthened in the faith and grew daily in numbers."

Please make special note that the church's outward mission is accomplished by means of its inner development. Edification, if it truly occurs, leads to evangelization, but evangelism by itself does not necessarily result in edification.

In church life, discipleship counseling is essential. The eldership of the church does not function here instead of the believers; rather, elders enable the believers to grow into their ministries. When numerical growth comes primarily from the efforts of skilled staff persons, church obesity results. It is far better when mature members are accountable for the increased birth rate. That way, the breasts that feed are always close by the womb that bears.

## 2. Using Scripture to Distinguish between Merely Human Ideas and Divine Imperatives

God alone has the right to determine how the body of his Son is to be structured and how it is to function. Churches around the world, however, differ on so many things. How can we sort out this confusion?

On issues where God has not spoken, differences may properly exist so long as there is no infringement on other biblical principles. On issues of the church and its life, where God has spoken, everyone is obligated to comply. Figure 5 is a visual aid I have used for years in resolving often-heated conflicts.

**The New Testament "5-22" Balance**

Figure 5

The figure expresses a simple plan for looking at the New Testament that will help in deciding between differing views about the church and its practices. I quote from my book *Healing for the Church:*

> There are twenty-seven books in the New Testament, and the simple diagram indicates that the first five books, which are history, are to be interpreted by the remaining twenty-

201

two books that make up the testament. Matthew, Mark, Luke, John, and Acts tell the story and show the various activities of our Lord and the apostles. While it is true that much basic teaching is given in the parables, sermons, and recorded experiences, it is also true that we may not safely ignore God's own interpretations, which follow in the remainder of the New Testament. For example, it is improper for one to point to a happening in the narrative section of the New Testament and make that activity obligatory for our day. Even if Jesus is shown spending much time on the open road walking about in sandals, that does not mean that each faithful minister must do the same!

When God expects us to make something in the first five books our literal, permanent model, it will be clear enough in the instructions and seen in the church practice delineated in the final twenty-two books. The Epistles are given for that very purpose of enlightenment. Here then are three safe standards for interpreting Scripture on this vital subject of the church:

1. *Each* basic essential for church life is revealed in Scripture.
2. *Nothing* may be made basic and essential unless it is revealed in Scripture as being basic and essential.
3. *Everything* revealed as basic and essential must be treated as such, with full obedience.

Two further observations need to be made. First, it is impossible to argue conclusively from the Bible's silence on any subject. Trying to establish or condemn a teaching or practice on the basis of what Scripture does not say is quite unsound.

Second, a principle of flexibility must be employed when considering church structure. Even in Bible days the assemblies were not all exactly alike. Considerable freedom in the worship and organization was present. Yet, I take it that the three standards mentioned in connection with [fig. 5] above were surely followed as the young churches developed. The Epistles gave them special guidance. (pp. 16-17)

No one dares think lightly of these matters. Scripture shakes us awake to their profound importance when it reveals that God, who created all things, has a specific, eternal purpose in mind for the church that goes far beyond any interests we might have for "our" church: "His intent was that now, through the church, the manifold wisdom of God should be made known to the rulers and authorities in the heavenly realms, according to his eternal purpose which he accomplished in Christ Jesus our Lord" (Eph. 3:10-11).

## 3. Using Part 1 to Measure the Separation of Churches from Their Head

Our study of the church is very much a part of the whole thrust of this book. In this second part, we have been studying evidence of great doctrines (of the person and work of Jesus Christ) being slighted or set aside as believers practice and apply their faith as best they can. Let's begin our inquiry into the separation of the churches from the Head by studying how some basic truths are viewed and applied in today's churches. Sadly, the failures we are to look at shape life in modern churches and, in some instances, give every indication that we have to a serious degree "lost connection with the Head, from whom the whole body, supported and held together by its ligaments and sinews, grows as God causes it to grow" (Col. 2:19). How is the doctrine of Christ's headship faring?

## The Meaning of Jesus' Headship

The Epistle to the Ephesians shows us that the church's life and well-being are inextricably dependent upon its Head. Paul closes chapter 1 with these words: "And God placed all things under his feet and appointed him to be head over everything *for the church*, which is his body, the fullness of him who fills everything in every way" (vv. 22-23).

This means that the Lord who is now established as sovereign Ruler of all powers and authorities of the universe is the One who, in love, is given to the church as its glorious Head. We now see that the designation "Head" is applied to Christ as official Ruler of all things in the universe. The term is also used in an intimate, organic sense when he is said to be Head of the church, as his body. The universe is not his body; the church is. How we view the church, his body, will be determined by our understanding of, and submission to, the Head. Surely the Lord Jesus Christ has spoken much about, and to, his churches. Our plans for our own local church must be prayerfully checked with the church's exalted Head. Furthermore, our life and service must show the dynamic of Christ's personal presence filling his body.

The words "in Christ" stand out in bold relief when joined to "the church." All the mighty truths of part 1 converge on this new creation of God, his holy people. Adam and his total family line have been disqualified; Christ and his new family line have been qualified. "The Father . . . has qualified you to share in the inheritance of the saints in the kingdom of light" (Col. 1:12).

This exalted destiny is based upon believers' change in lineage and headship. "For as in Adam all die, so in Christ all will be made alive" (1 Cor. 15:22). Among all nations of earth, those who believe are counted in Christ; that is, he is their Head. Together, all those in Christ make up the church, his body. The church is also called the bride of Christ and God's building, or temple.

But do we carefully, humbly, and obediently manifest these teachings? When members of the church convene in planning sessions, is Jesus Christ in charge? Is it his directions that are being followed? Surely the Head has not dictated the confusing, conflicting differences that so often occur within and between our local fellowships. Perhaps it seems old fashioned and not quite up to modern pace to resort to much prayer—and even fasting—in order to make sure that the decisions we make line up with orders gotten from our Head. But in the disregard of such practices lies one root of our problems.

## Conspiracy of Silence?

Consider next our Lord's incarnation, his humiliation. The very meaning of the name "Jesus" ("the Lord will save") is intended to establish the fact that he is the Savior from sin. He tells us that he came to seek and save lost and sinful human beings. His human life was poured out to show the way out of sin, and he died to provide redemption from sin. Just before he ascended to heaven, Jesus passed on the order to the apostles that "repentance and forgiveness of sins will be preached in his name to all nations" (Luke 24:47). In the light of this major emphasis on sin, how may we explain the silence of the contemporary church on this very subject?

Implications of the doctrine of universal depravity are vast. People of every culture found anywhere in the world today, or during any age of all history, stand in need of salvation, correction by the Word of God, and a steady ministry of the transforming grace of God. As we have already shown, Christ's plan of rescue changes the spiritual status of human beings from the sinful lineage of Adam to the family of our Savior, Jesus Christ. This is the first and fundamental step of salvation.

Consider, then, how serious is the loss of the doctrine of sin. Our diluted message has not corrected our own sinful culture; instead, our culture has invaded and corrupted our churches. Not only is the subject of sin neglected in preaching and teaching, but this omission also has allowed sin in many forms to weave a web of immorality deep within the vitals of churches.

For example, human marriage is intended to be a primary picture of the union of Christ and believers. Our Lord, then, must be grieved deeply when pastors and leaders of his flock allow the high value of marriage to be tarnished by the growing numbers of men and women who have "live-in" girlfriends or boyfriends. Observe the sad story too often told by successive issues of church directories—cohabitations in migration and the swapping of marriage partners. Other partners have strayed and dropped out of sight without strong recovery efforts being made. How poorly this moral confusion reflects on the church's Head! If he is not to be blamed (and he is not!), then has not the body drifted from the presence and control of the Lord Christ?

Furthermore, once the sanctity of marriage has been erased and our "rights" have taken precedence over God's rights and what he declares is right for the church, it becomes difficult to say that any adulterous and deviant unions are wrong. The preaching becomes muted with a kind of laryngitis. But "the wicked freely strut about when what is vile is honored among men" (Ps. 12:8). Scripture, however, plainly addresses the matter: "Do not be deceived: Neither the sexually immoral nor idolaters nor adulterers nor male prostitutes nor homosexual offenders nor thieves nor the greedy nor drunkards nor slanderers nor swindlers will inherit the kingdom of God" (1 Cor. 6:9). Is this the message that is proclaimed in public preaching and practiced in pastoral care?

Related to this loss is the widespread ignorance of *propitiation*—ignorance of what this grand word means and how its truth is extensively woven into our faith. When propitiation is set forth, we are faced with the utter helplessness of our sinful condition: the gospel declares that it is impossible for us to contribute anything toward removing sin's immense guilt and gaining God's approval. Jesus Christ alone must square the debt and bring us out into the light of his freedom.

The church must major in expounding this truth, winning men and women to it, and helping parents to make it clear to their children. "Jesus Christ and him crucified" (1 Cor. 2:2) is to be the theme of the Christian's witness everywhere. But is this really happening? Why is it that children and young people (and adults) within the churches do not understand the very truth upon which their eternal destiny depends? Furthermore, is it right that broken and despairing individuals pass through the steps of pastoral care and are referred to outside specialists without ever being shown how the atonement might play a role in their recovery?

Indeed, the church must again blaze with the light of its Head in glory: Jesus Christ *there* for us, and we *here* for him, standing in his name and experiencing the personal fullness of his Spirit. Through this means, our own church fellowships can throb with the very life of heaven. Our Lord will not absent himself from such a fellowship.

## 4. Examples from Contemporary Church Life

God's ideas for the church differ from our ideas: "For my thoughts are not your thoughts, neither are your ways my ways," declares the Lord. "As the heavens are higher than the earth, so are my ways higher than your ways and my thoughts than your thoughts" (Isa. 55:8-9). These words ring with needed warning when one looks at how we have designed and proceeded to practice church life today.

The best of human reasoning within the contemporary church argues with conviction that intense personal tragedies and brokenness are most often beyond the capacities of the church to help. We have already mentioned how needy ones commonly go outside for help, or perhaps they are committed to professionals and institutions. We have backed off so far from dealing with problems that, in some cases, we now support by fees and taxes what might have been provided freely from within the church.

## Shepherds Tend the Sheep

Pastors are shepherds, and shepherds tend the flock. The flock is made up of individual sheep. Hurt sheep may not always be expected to cooperate with the shepherd's appointment book, lining up in orderly fashion at the office door. Jesus spoke of the shepherd risking his life to rescue his own sheep, or even leaving ninety-nine sheep and going after a lost one. Mutual caring for one another is often so alien to life in the average church that special seminars and courses must be interjected and special organizational structures arranged to sustain what should arise normally from the Bible's picture of the church and Christian life.

After more than ten years under psychiatric care and various forms of counseling therapies, Sharon was worse, not better. Morning worship service had ended, and she needed help in finding her way to the parking lot, a simple and familiar route even to children. I led her to her waiting family and arranged with her husband to discuss her future.

Sharon's problem predated by a good many years the beginning of my ministry at the church, but only after her family's decision was made to accept and surround her with the full ministries of the church did I discover the spiritual roots of her difficulties. Her troubled behavior was definitely connected with skewed doctrine, which in turn had given a further, more direct opening to Satan. She was indeed a plagued person. Today she is free and able to minister to her own family and other wives and mothers of the church. Contributing to her enlightenment and recovery were the following church ministries: personal discipling for her and for her husband, pastoral counseling for both of them, nourishment of the whole family through neighborhood church meetings, and growth through public teaching beamed at real-life situations.

If pastoring means only administrating and preaching, what will become of the sheep with critical needs? And they are many in number. Some churches hire staff members who are specially trained to counsel, disciple, visit the elderly and infirm, work with youth—indeed, to do all the things the body itself ought to do. Other churches distribute their needy, hurting ones to community services or trained clinicians, who offer a regimen of drugs and counseling that jump-starts them and then serves as emotional scaffolding to enable them to continue functioning. Pastors, though, ought to lead the way in soul care and also go the next step as well: training and involving others in this ministry. The multiplication of discipleship counselors lies at the heart of a healthy church.

## Churches Need Not Back Off
Another major manifestation of human wisdom redesigning

church life occurs when members of churches get together, apart from their churches, and plan how to meet needs at home and abroad. They could gather as representatives of their church or of their churches, but they generally seem not to consider that option. Deep in the heart of average Christians is the thought that their church is somehow in a permanent disconnect with the needs of their community and world and that intermediary structures and organizations must therefore be devised to meet those needs.

Once people disappear into prisons, mental hospitals, military bases, and universities, or even when they enter certain professions, they become like the multitudes hidden in distant lands. Church people don't see them or touch them directly, except for the select few members who form the organizations raised up to conduct independent missions to those special groups. Outside their churches these leaders take up various burdens as their specialization. Granted, the organizations are made up of church people, but they are usually not there as delegates of their church. The local church is of course often involved through appeals for money, prayer, and personnel. These good works would be even better, however, if local churches were more involved in the decisions or, better yet, if the church could be trained to assume the ministries in two ways: *direct service of the local body* in ministries located within their reach, and *indirect ministry* by commissioning and sending members of their fellowship to more distant regions.

Here are several examples of how one of the churches I served moved directly into local opportunities:

1. *Military base.* A number from a nearby military base attended our meetings. They were enlisted to spearhead visitation through the barracks. On-base Bible studies,

hospitality in the homes of church families, and our main discipling ministry gave impetus to our outreach to the military.

2. *University campus.* Our church prepared and commissioned members of our fellowship who were students at a nearby institution to move through the dorms, witnessing for Christ and seeking prospects for Bible study.

3. *Prison.* Men of the church went regularly to visit inmates and hold Bible studies. When one believed, arrangements were made for baptism at our church.

4. *Hospitals and convalescent homes.* I remember on one Sunday afternoon being questioned by a patient I did not know. After I had completed a brief visit with a believer in the next bed, this man responded to my passing greeting with, "How many ministers do you have down there at your church? You're the third one this afternoon to come in here to the other bed, carrying a Bible and praying!" It was good to learn that one of the neighborhood shepherds I had trained was functioning and that he had in turn prepared one of his flock to enter the work as well.

My purpose here is to say that churches are made up of people who live scattered throughout the community, and they also work and attend school among the very citizens whom believers are to reach for God. Two common mistakes of churches in this matter of outreach are to back away from open doors, giving funds to have trained outsiders move into the areas of opportunity, or to enlarge the church staff to meet developing needs. In either case, the body of believers is trained to be inert, concentrating on giving money and doing tasks only within the church precincts.

## What Orders for Church Music?

According to figure 5, referred to earlier in this chapter, it is not enough to say that a particular way of worshiping or ministering is necessary for us to pursue simply because it appears in the historical accounts of the Bible. Here is the real question: is a particular manner of worshiping or ministering *assigned* to the church? Ornate worship in the Old Testament or even certain practices described in the historical accounts of the New Testament are not obligatory for the church. For example, we see the first new believers in Acts selling property and forming a common treasury. As we read on into the Epistles, however, where instructions are given to the early church, a common treasury is not there. Please review the earlier material on "The New Testament '5-22' Balance" and see the rationale for saying that no one can make anything *essential* for the church if God's own orders to the church do not so specify it. Beware of arguing from the silence on a matter.

The force and shrillness of arguments today over music in the church stand in marked contrast to the almost complete absence of New Testament prescription regarding music for the church meetings. We are making specific choices regarding music to be something that the apostles neither practiced nor commanded. It is not enough to make a case built on the beauty and antiquity of psalm singing. Then, shall the giftedness and godliness of Isaac Watts and the Wesleys affect our decision making? And what about Handel's *Messiah,* supported by a great organ—is that not heavenly? But are we clearly *commanded* to have it so?

At the other end of the church-music spectrum, I can well remember when organs were first being set aside for guitars and drums, and many choir robes hung unused as singers preferred jeans and miniskirts. Here again we must ask the question: are we clearly *obligated* in Scripture to worship using this more informal style?

Since so little about music is mandated in Scripture for the church, we must seek to find out whether there are underlying roots to this contemporary tension that do in fact violate God's Word. Let me give a brief warning to those positioned at each extreme. Regarding the formal style, I remember my father once balking at going to a particular church's worship service. They had a robed choir, a powerful organ, stained glass windows, an eloquent preacher—but, complained Dad, "I'm afraid to scratch my ear when I'm in there." The icy clutches of empty formalism can quench freedom of worship. Something is wrong if that happens.

In contrast, a music presentation that involves self-promoting strutting seems more in keeping with the culture of the age than with Scripture. The Pastoral Epistles describe in considerable detail the manner that befits God's servants, particularly those who minister in the assembly of believers.

## Getting Up Front

Aside from looking at the issue of music style, we need to inquire how the whole issue of "up front on the stage" got into the life of a local church. Ambitious parents now vie to get their children "up front." Some have confided to me their grief for their children because "they just can't do anything in front of people." Such a focus is foreign to our biblical orders from Headquarters.

Nor has the pastoral role escaped these same currents of custom. In most churches, the role of pastor does not primarily mean "pastor-ing," or engaging in the soul-care of believers in the fellowship. More emphasis is usually placed on preaching and administrative leadership. Again, such an idea of the pastor's task has to do with the up-front orientation, aimed at attracting a growing attendance. As people drive by a spacious church building, they say, "That is where Dr. Smith preaches" or "There is Pastor Jones's church."

The fallout from this emphasis is there to be seen just beneath the surface of all the programmed action. The body is not building itself up in loving ministries to one another. Too often members serve to gain numbers and build up programs, but the programs fail to get all the attendees into a life of discipling and edifying one another.

## What Are We Exporting?

I was shocked to learn that most of the young pastors seated before me under the palm-tree canopy at the jungle's edge were unemployed. This information changed my teaching emphasis very abruptly. The missionaries sponsoring this conference in Latin America were cooperating with the seminary from which the young men were graduated. Here they sat in conference around the tables, while scattered over the region were little companies of unshepherded believers. In some cases empty church buildings stood in silent judgment of the infectious ailment imported by the missionaries from their homeland.

Without exception, each man had grown up in very humble circumstances, including homes with mud floors, where chickens wandered in and out of their sleeping and eating areas. But subsidized schooling in nice buildings with tiled floors retrained their tastes and ideas of living standards. The former cobbler with several children now required a significant salary before he would consider moving into a community. The biblical concept of a church with a plurality of elders who remain in the work force until their ministry proves itself and demands its own remuneration was not considered.

In another Latin American country, I sensed that the earnest leading elder did not seem to be in a close unity with his wife. With a missionary translating for me, I conversed with the pastor and his wife together, asking for the privilege of speaking frankly and begging their pardon, since I might not have another such opportunity. "Please tell us whatever God would have you say," he responded most humbly.

"Do you and your wife pray regularly together with a true freedom?" I asked.

*(hesitation)* "We always pray together as a family at each meal."

"But do you and your wife pray together regularly and with freedom?"

"Well, sometimes we have the children offer the prayer of thanks."

*(missionary translator growing anxious)* "You still have not answered my question," I said as gently as I could.

With bowed head, he admitted, "No, we do not pray together."

"May I now offer this challenge to you? The believers here make up a local body of Christ, and no one in this body is closer to you than your spouse. If you are the upper arm in the body, then your wife must be the forearm. It is not possible for you to share a greater flow of vitality with more-distant members than you pass to your wife. A tourniquet between the two of you will limit your ministry to the more-distant ones in your fellowship."

The good pastor readily repented in prayer and surrendered himself to a new life of headship and personal ministry to his wife and family, and to the church. An unexpected schedule change brought me back into that city again on a Sunday. This same elder presided over a very meaningful Communion service. Hurrying outdoors afterward, he caught up with me on the sidewalk and reported with deep emotion that God was at work in a new way in his marriage and family.

A concluding word: Schooling and discipling of church leaders—yes, even of regular believers in a church—should always include inquiry into their marriage relationship and training in this crucial area, as in the example above. Otherwise, church life will sink to the level of its leaders' private lives. A costly expenditure of energy and funds to keep programs operating will perhaps hide the unrealness for a time, but any fruit that might appear will not last into other generations.

## Which Book Determines Things?

"You don't understand our culture. We could never practice what you are teaching!" objected one of the pastors in the mountains of a Central American country. I was leading a pastor's conference for a dedicated band of men serving in isolated villages scattered over the steep terrain. They spoke various local dialects, but all were fluent in Spanish and wished me to know that they all were decidedly Indian in their culture. I already knew that, of course, so I went to great lengths to launder out the suspicion that I wanted them to be North American. Indeed, some of their church practices were superior to those followed in the States.

After showing Scriptures that urge us to be faithful to one another in correcting and strengthening or personally edifying and discipling (Acts 20:20-31; Col. 1:28-29; 3:16; 1 Thess. 2:11-12; 5:11, 14; Heb. 3:12-13, and others), I urged them to dedicate themselves to this ministry. Although in disciplining fallen believers they were bold almost to the point of brutality (or at least that is how it would appear to us in North America), they still balked at the notion of using Scripture in the service of personal discipling. After making sure I had laid a clear and biblical basis for my admonition, I proceeded in this fashion: "You have a book of culture that says, 'Do things *this* way.' Here is God's Book. It says, 'Do things *that* way.' You must choose which book you will follow in this matter."

At a later, very solemn final service of dedication, one of the highly regarded senior men addressed the conferees in an exceptionally moving manner, saying, "I have been wrong in my ways of ministry. God's Word has corrected me, and I now return home to begin over anew, and in the right way."

### 5. What about House Churches?

Without a doubt, "church" means different things to different people in our modern world:

1.  A congregation with salaried staff pastors who conduct most or all of the ministry themselves. *or*

2.  A congregation taught by staff pastors, with the aim that ministries are done as each member exercises his or her gifts. This approach will likely be supported by a plan of leadership development. *or*

3.  A congregation from which numbers of persons are developed by the pastoral team as spiritual leaders, to serve as elders and shepherds. The staff pastors thus reproduce themselves by training others who can guide the whole body into a fruitful life of ministry.

Only the third view of the church brings the essential and gradual structural alterations that lead to true permanence. The congregation becomes self-sustaining and protected from the endless cycle of reinfection of old faulty traditions. Instead of being reliant on pastors who are "hired in," the church busies itself in producing its own leaders. Institutional training might indeed have a part in that preparation and might be needed to supplement what the church's pastors and teachers can provide. Pastors who truly know what they are doing in ministry should be able to lead others to know and practice the same. In brief, we should all study to reproduce ourselves as far as possible.

A purposeful emphasis on reproduction of those who fill the biblical offices and devote themselves to shepherding God's people will require a form of life that can employ the increasing number of leaders in vital ministries. Such a regular preparation and production of leaders will fit quite normally with a proper vision of shepherding people in the neighborhoods where they reside. We thus are led to a consideration of neighborhood churches—that is, house churches.

## The Earliest Churches—in Homes

By the term "house church," I mean something quite different from home fellowships, prayer and share groups, home Bible studies, and the like. The biblical expression "the church that meets at their house" (Rom. 16:5), referring here to the residence of Priscilla and Aquila, means that this couple hosted an identifiable segment of the larger church at Rome. Evidence seems to indicate that a very substantial company of elders led the church, but no evidence exists from the first century of a building large enough to accommodate the sizable congregation gathered from the whole city. Did not the church at Rome (as well as larger city congregations elsewhere) meet more often in neighborhood churches and then, when possible, gather for whole-church meetings either in rented quarters or outdoors?

Early house churches, as replicas of the whole city church, were ideally pastored by elders. Study Romans 16:3-5, 1 Corinthians

16:19, Colossians 4:15-16, and Philemon 1-2. Neighborhood house churches afford rich and immediate opportunities for full expression of spiritual gifts by each participant. Each person serves, and each one receives ministry from the others.

Two objections are commonly heard against implementing this concept of the local church in our day. First is the concern over a breakdown in the unity of the larger church. If the plan is carried out in a proper fashion, however, it really should promote unity. Rifts will be more quickly noticed and dealt with because the unified team of pastors, or elders, are serving right among the people, close to home.

Another reservation about granting full status to a church in a home has to do with worry over a breakdown in authority in the citywide church. Again, if done right, the plan will actually promote and safeguard the unified authority of the eldership and congregation. Given a body of elders functioning in line with Paul's instruction to the collective eldership of Ephesus ("Keep watch over yourselves and all the flock," Acts 20:28), any emergence of a presumptuous individualism will be exposed soon enough to prevent widespread harm.

A bit of reflection will show that those in the biblical offices must be qualified in character, prepared by training, and manifesting an unwavering commitment to the whole assembly. Members of the various neighborhood churches will be more involved and committed than they would have been if they worshiped only in the large congregational meetings.

In those places today where church planting is begun with a first house church, then, as growth requires, a second one, and so on until perhaps there are several, the unified congregational meetings—whenever they occur—will be very special. In contrast, when the usual weekly practice is a congregational gathering in a commodious sanctuary, then any church meeting in a home will be special or unusual and will require much attention and preparation.

## Consider the Advantages

Recall the three basic functions of a church: worship, edification, and extension. Consider how the form of multiplied house churches will impact each function. The neighborhood emphasis in pastoring and shepherding will allow a higher level of participation in the worship and a deeper commitment to individual discipling and to more intensive ministries that build up the body.

Still further, in a house church the way is immediately opened for a new emphasis on evangelism. Dreamed of but seldom seen is evangelism *by* the church, instead of evangelism *in* the church building. The former is more easily fostered out in the neighborhoods through the house churches than it is when limited to the large, central congregation.

Above and beyond the vision of gathering new people into the house church, each neighborhood assembly must conceive of itself as a movement, not a dead end. The church in the home is a means of multiplying into other neighborhood fellowships. However, if this concept is not carefully inculcated from the outset, the people will settle down into a much loved but selfish fellowship. The thought of dividing from one another will seem unbearable and unreasonable. If dealt with properly, though, the expansion will be accepted as a solemn responsibility, and this discipline and commitment will in turn make the large congregational meetings very powerful and joyful, as old friends and new believers mingle.

The scope of this book does not permit discussion of further details of house church life and ministry, but I should make it clear that, if preparations are carefully made and executed with much prayer, a bona fide church in the home, led by elders functioning as part of the main church, will provide its members with a depth of spiritual experience and challenge in service that will be beyond any other small-group setting. In the latter, the people *meet* together; in the former, they *live* together. Picture the fathers and mothers and children of a neighborhood gathering each week. It is an intergenerational meeting. Not only do the children know each other, but they see their own dads and their friends' dads leading their gatherings. Expectant mothers may be a part of such meetings. All celebrate together with each new birth, physical and spiritual. Family values are best taught in such a family setting.

## 6. Concluding Thoughts

The opening chapters of Revelation reach out to us with strong encouragement. There we are introduced to churches with all kinds of faults, but the Lord Jesus is shown standing among them. He had not abandoned any of the seven churches. Take, for example, the church in Laodicea, to whom he spoke the following:

> You say, "I am rich; I have acquired wealth and do not need a thing." But you do not realize that you are wretched, pitiful, poor, blind and naked. I counsel you to buy from me gold refined in the fire, so you can become rich; and white clothes to wear, so you can cover your shameful nakedness; and salve to put on your eyes, so you can see. Those whom I love I rebuke and discipline. So be earnest, and repent. Here I am! I stand at the door and knock. If anyone hears my voice and opens the door, I will come in and eat with him, and he with me. (Rev 3:17-20)

Imagine it—the Head of the church asking to be allowed entrance to one of his churches! Our heart doors and church doors must be opened wide to the Lord, even as one day we shall look and long for his door to open to us when "the wedding of the Lamb has come, and his bride has made herself ready" (Rev. 19:7).

As a bride prepares herself with great care and eagerness for the approaching wedding, she has one paramount thought, "What will my loved one think of this apparel, of that adornment?" Let us cease arguing, "This program has served well over years!" or "That approach gets more community attention!" Our Lord has not hidden his preferences concerning the church. Indeed, "it was he who gave some to be apostles, some to be prophets, some to be evangelists, and some to be pastors and teachers, to prepare God's people for works of service, so that the body of Christ may be built up until we all reach unity in the faith and in the knowledge of the Son of God and become mature, attaining to the whole measure of the fullness of Christ" (Eph. 4:11-13).

All members of each church are responsible to share in preparing for the Marriage. We are ordered to "encourage one another daily, as long as it is called Today, so that none of you may be hardened by sin's deceitfulness" (Heb. 3:13).

Familial terms are frequently used in Scripture to describe God's relationship to us. These expressions point us to our highest possible levels of spiritual life. Addressing God as our Father, thinking of ourselves as his children, and, beyond that, living as a bride awaiting the return of her Lord should lift us far beyond attempting to fix or fashion the church according to our own notions.

Furthermore, this elevated view of our church as Christ's bride will stir us to diligence in keeping the assembly pure from immorality. For instance, adultery and broken marriages are a double injury to our Head. Marital sin not only vitiates the image of Christ and his bride, but it also directly mars the Lord's bride herself, for that is what the local church is, and marriages and families are an essential portion of the church. Ponder again these words: "For the husband is the head of the wife as Christ is the head of the church, his body, of which he is the Savior. . . . Husbands, love your wives, just as Christ loved the church and gave himself up for her to make her holy, cleansing her by the washing with water through the word, and to present her to himself as a radiant church, without stain or wrinkle or any other blemish, but holy and blameless" (Eph. 5:23-27).

Christ's bride, the church, is also disfigured when his followers redesign her after their own ideas or traditions—as I have sought to show in this chapter. One distressful contemporary example of this disfigurement consists in the loss of discipleship counseling from the church's life. This defect derives from widespread weakening of both planned and spontaneous edification, or discipling, between individual believers.

Key to the entire regression is the redefining of the pastoral role. Numbers of powerful, leader-type pastors use their superior skills to move their organization along with machine-like precision, and throngs of admirers are attracted by the momentum of lively programs. Other ministers are expert at orchestrating a boundless enthusiasm and joyful participation in the public meetings. In either case, the results are perhaps too much contrived and too easily explained. That is, the output is commensurate with the input. In the mix of invested "means" to the ends are faithful committees, a complement of staff and volunteer workers, adequate finances, and tireless, energetic leadership of a skilled senior person or a visionary top team.

These examples, however, seem much in contrast with our Lord's description of his plan for production of fruit. The good seed in prepared soil increases by as much as a hundredfold. In Mark 4 this familiar parable is strengthened by the addition of a second: "This is what the kingdom of God is like. A man scatters seed on the ground. Night and day, whether he sleeps or gets up, the seed sprouts and grows, though he does not know how. All by itself the soil produces grain—first the stalk, then the head, then the full kernel in the head. As soon as the grain is ripe, he puts the sickle to it, because the harvest has come" (vv. 26-29).

A stubborn, headstrong individualism easily misses orders from the church's Lord. Hundreds of thousands of "true believers" are marching out and away from local church involvement with heads held high, in spite of the clear example of Jesus Christ in the first three chapters of Revelation. He does not abandon his imperfect assemblies.

Those who loyally remain with their church must ask themselves, Are the distinctives for which I argue and stand set forth and argued for in Scripture? Am I reinventing the church based on my judgment of "what works" and is more attractive? Finally, ask, Have I marginalized, or even missed, plain commands to the church? True, some things are left unsaid in Scripture, and these matters are ours to work out by prayerful planning and diligent execution. But whatever Jesus Christ has revealed as his way for the church, we are obligated to carry out fully. Our own ventures must never conflict with the directions of Scripture.

Jesus' words to the Pharisees and teachers of the law might well apply to some of today's church leaders: "You have let go of the commands of God and are holding on to the traditions of men" (Mark 7:8).

## Where Do We Go from Here?

Two certainties must be held in mind. First, God is not yet finished. Second, whenever something God promises seems to fail, the fault is on earth, not in heaven. Precisely here is the burden of this book—to declare that the confusion of discordant sights and sounds, as well as the loss of power, is based ultimately on a drifting from fundamental truth. When precious revelation that is committed to the church is not cherished, pored over, and made ever clearer through faithful teaching, the presence of the Lord Jesus Christ, the Head of the church, begins to be crowded out as human devices take over.

## Two Calls

First, *the call to action.* Only one thing is worse than trying to supplant the devil without planting the church: trying to plant the church without supplanting the devil. How grotesque is that enterprise called a church in which Satan is not displaced! The more he is able to coexist with what is thought of as acceptable form and doctrine, the worse it is.

There must therefore be a breaking down as well as a building up—a casting out as well as an infilling. Those who avoid the negative dimension of a call to recovery will not arrive at God's plan to establish his holy temple. Practices that contravene Scripture must cease, even if the change is painful and involves removal of white-haired tradition or things cherished and popular.

The crucial issue, however, is how this correction shall be accomplished. This concern leads to a second call: the *call to caution.* A trustworthy principle for making change within a church might be stated in this way: When a practice is not implicitly evil, never attack it or even attempt to close it down until you have a better thing already in place and thriving. Then simply let life replace death.

Some might suppose that I am issuing a call here to radical change in outward structure. Going the route toward "No large buildings!" or "No professional clergy!" however, will not purge infections and deliver the modern church from its ills. New life for the church is not to be sought by hasty human action that merely adjusts the outward form of the church. What the Lord Christ designs and calls into existence must reveal what he is like and what he likes. Such serious considerations will be clear only to those who have earnestly and fully repented of their way of living thoughtlessly with what they "grew up with." Or perhaps repentance will be in order because of a blind acceptance of whatever kind of church one happened upon in one's particular experience.

In the opening chapters of Revelation, Jesus did not speak vaguely and generally to Christendom; rather, he spoke very personally to each of the seven churches. To the Ephesian church he said, "If you do not repent, I will come to you and remove your lampstand from its place" (Rev. 2:5).

## A Sobering Word

Critiquing the bride of Christ is a serious, even dangerous, undertaking: "If anyone destroys God's temple, God will destroy him; for God's temple is sacred, and you are that temple" (1 Cor. 3:17). May God therefore be merciful toward this writer, as well as any readers who undertake a response to what has been written.

Jesus halted men from stoning the adulterous woman. Shall we rush to throw rocks at our Lord's bride? Instead, let us with gentle touch straighten—if necessary—the hem of her garment. And that can be done only on our knees.

# 14

# CONCLUSION: GETTING RID OF THE FACE AT THE WINDOW

The dark, shadowy figure is rarely seen but is sensed, leering and lurking about, prowling and scowling outside our window. At times we feel unsettled, but much of the time most of us live on in a kind of unsuspecting, dull unawareness. This is the way our great enemy Satan would have it.

Convincing Christians that we are being looked at, sized up, and misdirected is a difficult task. Please allow me to try.

To begin, here are three questions regarding what you may have experienced while working your way through this book. As you read part 1, did you find that all the teachings there were clear to you and being held firmly? (Being lax with truth and tight with Jesus is impossible.) Next, what did you learn from the Bible test found in appendix 6? Finally, were you helped in part 2 to see beneath the skin of things as you looked at the subjects of faith, prayer, evangelism, discipling, spiritual warfare, and church life today? Remember, our root problems are not merely the way churches are organized or their style of worship or weakness in written doctrinal statements—not even in what is proclaimed and counseled. If the Holy Spirit is not freely and fully at work, the form of these activities will never carry life.

We are nearing the end of our time together, and I would like to speak frankly. Our earlier discussions have turned up warning signs of significant problems—significant enough to keep our Lord at a distance from us. He now stands again at the door of our hearts and our churches, as he did at Laodicea. Again he insists, "*I know* your deeds" (Rev. 3:15), "but *you do not realize* that you are wretched, pitiful, poor, blind and naked" (v. 17). This blindness, I am convinced, has come about because truth has been slighted, the Spirit of Truth is grieved, and now Christ must be brought back.

Several verses later in the same chapter, we see Jesus outside our door and asking to come back in: "Here I am! I stand at the door and knock. If anyone hears my voice and opens the door, I will come in and eat with him, and he with me" (Rev. 3:20). This much-needed and wonderful reentering of the Lord into our lives and churches, in all his fullness, will most certainly require that the offenses first be cleared away. Undoubtedly, the offending actions and attitudes are both the cause and effect, the root and result, of laxness with the doctrines we have been discussing in this book.

Much reflection on our modern church condition has led me to conclude that there are three major areas of sin that are grieving our Lord and holding him at a distance from us. Though, as Jesus warned above, "You do not realize [it]," many of the very ones who claim to be Christians, even spiritual leaders, have yielded to these evils.

1. *Immorality and impurity.* Inattention to vital truth always holds hands with personal sin and moral compromise. We can only imagine the number of prominent Christians of our day

who are privately entertained by the dramatization of the very sins they claim to stand against. Lounging on their couches before TV at home or intensely perusing the Internet, they sip from the Babylonian harlot's cup. They trade spiritual vigor for evil gratification. Now they must compensate for this loss by substituting humanly designed efforts at home and in the church. Where is Christ in all this?

The grand concept of grace has been distorted in the subconscious thought of many, with the result that "grace" now provides safety for the dangerous life scripted by sinful passion. No! Grace provides for the life *God* designs, and God is holy. God's true children "are led by the Spirit of God" (Rom. 8:14). In that light, ask, Has the Holy Spirit ordered the life I am now living?

2. *Ambition and materialism.* Discussions involving salary, ownership of material things, retirement benefits and plans, professional fees and perks seem to flame with a more intense interest than those evoked by the truths covered in part 1. It is almost impossible, with human strength, to get one to admit that he or she is covetous. Lust is more readily admitted than greed. But God knows our hearts, and he calls materialism idolatry. The presence of Jesus is not to be found among such idols.

3. *Pride.* Here is the root. But the terrifying reality is that its existence is always denied unless the Holy Spirit brings enlightenment. One of sin's earliest damages is done to our equipment for making self-appraisal. In seeking to shake awake the Corinthians, who felt comfortable with their church, even though a case of immorality was known to be among them, the apostle's words came with searing heat: "And you are proud! Shouldn't you rather have been filled with grief and have put out of your fellowship the man who did this?" (1 Cor. 5:2). God

condemns those whose arms of fellowship embrace thieves and adulterers (Ps. 50:18).

Pride introduces the very spirit of the world into the church, and the Father's love withdraws: "Do not love the world or anything in the world. If anyone loves the world, the love of the Father is not in him. For everything in the world—the cravings of sinful man, the lust of his eyes and the boasting of what he has and does—comes not from the Father but from the world" (1 John 2:15-16).

Sadly, those most needing to hear these words are likely to pay the least attention. Revelation 3:17 warns exactly the ones who feel that they "do not need a thing." The prevailing attitude of such individuals regarding the truth is, "We've got it!"—rather than hungering and thirsting for needed enlightenment.

One simply must allow God's call to penetrate: "Your iniquities have separated you from your God; your sins have hidden his face from you, so that he will not hear" (Isa. 59:2). God charges, "They did not ask, 'Where is the Lord?'" (Jer. 2:6).

Perhaps some readers are holding steadfastly to the right doctrinal labels and to very familiar key phrases of Bible teaching. Years of unthinking handling of crucial teaching, however, have enabled them to say what sounds like solid truth to them and their unthinking hearers—but is it? Perhaps these persons are like Samson: "He did not know that the Lord had left him" (Judg. 16:20).

Have you held to cherished points of doctrine but lost the presence of Christ? If so, a thorough repentance will require admission of the pride that has made possible the continuing deception. Remember, "God opposes the proud but gives grace to the humble" (James 4:6).

Finally, a prayerful rereading of *Bringing Christ Back* might help put things right with God.

"Repent, then, and turn to God, so that your sins may be wiped out, that times of refreshing may come from the Lord, and that he may send the Christ, who has been appointed for you—even Jesus" (Acts 3:19-20).

# WHAT NOW?

If we acknowledge that we have grieved Jesus Christ, who is our Lord and Head, what do we do now?

Wonderful seasons of spiritual awakening and revival from past years might come to mind and call to us as a possibility for our own time. Perhaps our hearts are stirred by reports of believers in deep repentance turning from shallow and sinful living, and of unbelievers crowding into the kingdom. On the one hand, we see painful distress of soul over sins against our loving Lord, and on the other hand, widespread joy and celebration breaks out from those who truly repent. Accompanying these dramatic scenes is a powerful impact on both the church and the community. Churches are crowded, and a new regard for God and morality emerges in the public life.

## Two Unsettling Questions

Tucked away in those faithful hearts of past generations, and appearing in the diaries and records of these seasons of spiritual renewing, are frequent references to two deeply disturbing questions: Why the painfully long delays in the coming of revivals? And, Why the rapid decline in so many revivals?

May we dismiss these two pressing issues simply by saying that God is sovereign and that we must be more faithful in prayer? Both these suggestions are important, but what all too often is missing is a concurrence with God's eternal purposes in Christ Jesus our Lord.

## All for Our Head's Honor

When we cry out to God to restore the powerful presence of Christ to our lives and to our churches, we must desire more than the thrill of seeing sinners repenting, saints rejoicing, churches crowded, and communities changed. All these blessings must be prayed for *with reference to the honor of Christ enthroned in heaven.* We must plead for more than the longed-for mercy of God. We must, by prayer and our witness, open channels for Christ's rule to be extended here among us.

God first promised in Genesis 3:15 that a Deliverer, born from a human mother, would, at great cost to himself, overcome Satan. We are here introduced to the central theme of Scripture and the focus of divine purpose. Let us keep the focus in our praying. Again, take Psalm 110 as a guide when begging God to bring a reviving to your heart and to the church. With that Scripture as your guide, you will see Jesus Christ at God's right hand, and you will apply your prayers and efforts to break Satan's control over lives and the community, until all is as a footstool for the Messiah's feet. I see next in Psalm 110 that God purposes to extend the Savior's rule, even in the midst of his enemies (v. 2). Then, supporting these divine plans, is the promise of an encouraging, renewed interest on the part of the Lord's troops (v. 3).

Surely we have things backward when we pray for the renewal first. No, our foremost concern must be the honor of our glorious Lord—how that honor will be impacted by an outpouring of the Holy Spirit. This very order ought to be observed when we seek a new spiritual level for our personal lives. Rather than pleading first for a deeper life, a more victorious and surrendered life, we would do well to study prayerfully a Scripture like Colossians 3:1-4 and fix our attention first on who and what is *above*: "Since, then, you have been raised with Christ, set your hearts on things above, where Christ is seated at the right hand of God. Set your minds on things above, not on earthly things. For you died, and your life is now hidden with Christ in God. When Christ, who is your life, appears, then you also will appear with him in glory."

This bringing Christ back involves nothing less than all-out war. Once shamed and suffering, our Lord is now vindicated, honored, and adored in heaven. Our task is to share in bringing God's will to earth as it is in heaven, that the Son may be glorified. The great enemy Satan, however, has moved the center of his operations to earth, and we must contend with him. Our prayers for spiritual awakening will be more effective if they are focused not on me and my church but on the honor of Christ arising from each defeat of Satan in my life and in the life of my church.

## Changing Our Churches—a Must

As wondrous as so many episodes were during revival seasons of past history, woeful accounts have been written describing what came about in the years that followed. Take one example: a church signally blessed in the early American revivals, whose illustrious pastor stood in the vanguard of the awakening, began quarreling with its minister and ultimately discharged him! The problem was not with all the throngs of converts. Nor did these new ones quickly fall away. The problem was with the established churches and their pastors. These churches needed changing.

How essentially different are things today? If a large ingathering brings much more of what we already have— what then? To have and hold *new* life will require fundamental changes in the spiritual structure and life of the church. Intensive individual discipling must be provided to all leaders, regular members, and new converts. Leadership and ministries must be shared with all whom the Holy Spirit equips. A qualitative change—not just in the spirit and enthusiasm of the church but in the very way church life is practiced—will be needed if we are to welcome back our Lord Jesus Christ and continue to live with him.

> Lord, I have heard of your fame;
>> I stand in awe of your deeds, O Lord.
> Renew them in our day,
>> in our time make them known;
>> in wrath remember mercy.
>> (Hab. 3:2)

# APPENDIX 1

## DID GOD DIE ON THE CROSS?

The following paragraphs are taken from correspondence I wrote to a friend on whether it is correct to say that *God* died on the cross.

> I would caution you about using such expressions as "God died." God can neither lie nor die. Rather, give your energy to show that we sinners died in our Substitute's death. The Son took on a mortal nature that he might die. Because I am included in Christ's death, I am forgiven. This can be simply stated.
>
> Just as error might arise if one said, "God died at the cross," so error might arise if one said, "God did not die at the cross." The missing critical factor is the incarnation. That truth must be joined to either statement. Within the Trinity no alteration, change of any kind, is possible. But the greatest mystery of the universe is the incarnation, wherein the unchanging, holy, almighty God joined us— even becoming one of us. As with any miracle or supreme mystery, we ultimately stand at the outer edge of our limited knowledge and, in amazed silence, rely by faith on what is revealed to us.
>
> We know that no one can see God. He, in essence, is unseeable. But God can, in Jesus Christ, be seen [note John 14:8-9]. Our Savior is the image of the invisible God. He

not only could be seen, he could be tested, and he could hunger and weep, and he died.

Jesus Christ is the Son of God. The Son is God. Jesus Christ died for our sins. We know that. The critical issue is that Christ has two natures, but he is one in his person. He is divine in his person. This incarnation inextricably involves God in whatever Jesus did. "God was reconciling the world to himself in Christ" (2 Cor. 5:19). This act grows even more amazing when verse 19 is joined with 21.

As we stand in wonder at all this, we hear the cry from the cross, "My God, my God, why have you forsaken me?" (Matt. 27:46). Now rethink the question we are considering here. Our Lord, as man, died on the cross. Our Lord, as God, could not die.

Such is the nature of the incarnation that our Savior Jesus Christ, who is Deity, assumed a human nature and died as man without involving the eternal Godhead in change. This mystery is similar to saying that our omnipotent and omnipresent Lord could be hemmed in within Mary's womb. Or we might ask how an all-knowing God could also be an infant and need to learn. We worship a Lord who, regardless of the questions that may remain, perfectly bridges the God-man gap.

# Appendix 2

# The Salvation of Infants Who Die

Infants are subject to, liable to, death in both its phases: (1) inward corruption of character, and (2) physical death. The first phase of death is evident from the start of every individual life, requiring vigilance and diligence on the part of the parents to correct, restrain, and train. The second might come at any point from conception, during pregnancy, at birth, or afterward.

Since, according to Scripture, death is the penalty of sin, why do infants suffer death as described above? The answer is that they are in fact guilty. God does not condemn and punish the innocent. It is obvious also that a baby's lack of innocence cannot be judged from his or her countenance, because infants certainly have a precious, innocent appearance. Guilt refers to the state into which they are born, according to Romans 5:12. ("Therefore, just as sin entered the world through one man, and death through sin, . . . in this way death came to all men, because all sinned.") Adam has bequeathed damnation to the human family. The state of sin (legal guilt) is what we all inherit from Adam. Nor is this sin—as guilt—derived from sinful acts. No wrongdoing is present, of course, in the infant's behavior. The real problem is forensic, apart from breaking any law. Study carefully Romans 5:13-14: "For before the law was given, sin was

239

in the world. But sin is not taken into account when there is no law. [Infants are totally unaware of any law, thus their guilt does not come from lawbreaking.] Nevertheless, death reigned from the time of Adam to the time of Moses, even over those who did not sin by breaking a command, as did Adam."

Death as inner defilement and ultimately in the grave came to all those living after Adam and before the law came through Moses. The same is true for all unknowing babies. That is, a great universal taproot of sin exists, involving every breathing mortal, regardless of what he or she knows about right and wrong. This use of the term "sin" concerns God's judgment against the human family from the point of Adam's disobedience. Babies are born under the canopy of this legal condemnation, being under Adam's family headship, or "in Adam" (1 Cor. 15:22).

We come now to the major question at hand. If infants are thus declared guilty, what if they die in infancy? Can they be saved?

While all guilty persons could justly be condemned and lost from God, Scripture leads me to understand that infants are in fact saved when they die. The basis for their salvation is *not* that they are sweet and innocent in appearance, nor even that they have not yet done a wrong deed. Some just basis must be discovered that satisfies God and turns away judgment from guilty ones.

There is only one basis for salvation for anyone of any age, and that is through the Savior, Jesus Christ. What assurance have we that Jesus' blood atonement and righteousness is applied to the dying little one? Here are three lines of thought that should grant assurance to those who have this question.

First, in the biblical passages dealing with mankind's final judgment, the actual damnation is administered because of evil works. Notice this basis in such texts as John 5:28-29 and Revelation 20:12-13. In other words, the final conviction and punishment for sin will not be simply because one is related to Adam. This thought, however, does not prove that dying infants are saved; it merely says that Scripture does not in the judgment sections make us think that they are necessarily lost. But can they be saved?

Second, since infants have no record of wrongdoing that would bring them into damnation, they are fit candidates for the Savior's receiving them on the basis of pure grace alone.

Third, all depends on what the Sovereign Lord does with the little ones. If, as we have shown, nothing compels us to believe that infants will be condemned at the judgment, and if we understand that they might be saved by pure grace, then the only remaining question is, What did Jesus teach and demonstrate about children?

According to Jesus, the only persons with question marks of uncertainty over their eternal future are adults, not children. He said, "I tell you the truth, unless you change and become like little children, you will never enter the kingdom of heaven" (Matt. 18:3). Again, "The kingdom of heaven belongs to such as these [little children]" (Matt. 19:14).

In addition to Jesus' words recorded in the Gospels, other texts are relevant, such as 2 Samuel 12:23, where King David says of his deceased newborn son, "But now that he is dead, why should I fast? Can I bring him back again? I will go to him, but he will not return to me."

Perhaps we may also apply the principle disclosed in Isaiah 57:1, where those dying are said to be "spared from evil." We can well imagine that God's great broom of merciful grace sweeps a larger number into salvation from the nations with high rates of infant mortality than may be reached there through all our efforts in evangelism.

# APPENDIX 3

## THE PROBLEM OF EVIL IN GOD'S WORLD

If God, who is holy, is all-powerful, all-knowing, and everywhere present, then how did evil come into existence in a universe created by such a one? Many scholars have tackled this mystery. It is of the nature of all such ultimate questions that they present us with an unfathomable precipice and a divide. We stand on the edge looking out, but we don't see very far. We know God knows, and faith allows us to rest in what he has been pleased to tell us. Here are a few things I see in Scripture that build on what we looked into when we were defining the larger subject of sin.

*Evil's origin.* Let's trace sin back to a source. The visible occurrence of human sin, or *wrongdoing,* comes from the evil bias that contaminates our hearts. This *inner defilement*, as we have termed it, comes upon us as the penalty is passed on all Adam's family line when he sinned. Being thus in a state of *legal guilt*, Adam was punished with death—within and without, in heart and body.

Adam and Eve's interaction with Satan the tempter brought about a universal tragedy. In this interaction they accepted Satan's word in place of God's word. In consequence, the devil adopted Adam and Eve and their line as his own. The terribly serious aspect of this tragedy is that the human family is now cast under

Satan as "father."

This tragic relation is described in our Lord's teaching in John 8: "You belong to your father, the devil, and you want to carry out your father's desire. He was a murderer from the beginning, not holding to the truth, for there is no truth in him. When he lies, he speaks his native language, for he is a liar and the father of lies" (v. 44).

This text plainly lodges the ultimate beginning of evil in the person of Satan, who was the first to fall. Other Scriptures suggest that he fell from a considerable glory and now maintains a kind of princely jurisdiction over the whole world. Searching much beyond these facts will not answer all our questions. We learn of Satan's original pride and the like, but what were the parameters of his unfallen volition? We know that God did not make him stumble, and we know that God will one day turn all into his own honor. Perhaps this achievement will be God's masterpiece of might.

*Evil's extent.* Look again at the passage just quoted from John's gospel. Satan is seen there as more than a figurehead father. Human beings in their natural state are told by Jesus, "You belong to your father, the devil." The expression "belong to" means they are "of," or are "fathered by," this one who is intruding into God's place. Adam, then, became Satan's legal human representative to head up this universal family enterprise.

The real mystery is no longer how far evil has come but what restrains it. (See 2 Thess. 2:7.) In every mortal, evil flows and grows naturally. Our only rescue is to be reborn through Jesus Christ into God's true household. As we will see in chapters 3 and 4, the cross of Christ forever settles the dispute and opens the way to salvation.

*Evil's end.* The magnitude of history's final events has much to do with the nature of sin and its utter incorrigibility. Judicial guilt is without question established over all mankind. This condition means our banishment to a life in the grip of corrupting evil desires, which in turn leads to ever-increasing wrongdoing. Furthermore, the great superhuman Energizer of evil keeps the black tide flowing, and evil hearts resonate with his rule.

Readers are encouraged at this juncture to study Isaiah 26, noticing the manner of God's reign over his people and how the righteous respond to God's rule. But notice in verse 10 that the wicked react oppositely, according to their nature: "Though grace is shown to the wicked, they do not learn righteousness; even in a land of uprightness they go on doing evil and regard not the majesty of the Lord." Consider also all the divine efforts of the most powerful kind pictured in the Book of Revelation, from terrifying judgments to the glories offered in chapter 20. Through it all, mankind's sinful disposition proves to be incorrigible. Unless the guilt is removed, the penalty of death continues—within their characters and ultimately dragging all toward the grave and eternal destruction. Therefore, hell is both certain and eternal.

Seeing these truths, believers ought never cease praising God for the power and grandness of the redemption wrought by Jesus Christ, our Savior.

# Appendix 4

# Hope Heals Human Brokenness

Hope is a foundational—one could almost say, monumental—subject woven throughout Scripture. In addition to the many Bible texts that contain the word "hope," consider how many others, without use of the word itself, refer to or teach hope. More extensive than all these combined are the vast number of passages given to produce and foster hope within us.

Here I select some general aspects and a few specifics to suit our purpose as a supplement to our discussion in chapter 6. The aim of this addendum is to bring better definition to our understanding of hope and thus brighten its fire. Perhaps then we can hope to resist the chill winds Jesus warned of: "Because of the increase of wickedness, the love of most will grow cold" (Matt. 24:12).

Hope as a noun means "expectation." As a verb it might be translated "trust, expect, anticipate"—all with some degree of pleasure.

Faith and hope are partners. Though related, they are not identical. Perhaps it might be said that faith warms itself at hope's fireside and then provides the means of arriving at hope's goal.

Trouble is a familiar setting for hope. When thus surrounded, hope limits the shock of suffering. Indeed, believers are set apart from the world by their hope. Those separated from Christ are said to be "without hope" (Eph. 2:12). Faith in Christ thus brings one from no hope into "a living hope" (1 Peter 1:3).

God himself is our hope, help, trust, strength, and refuge. Those wanting to find a place of refuge in God must see themselves as refugees. Only then will they be candidates for the Holy Spirit's special work of communicating to needy ones all that the God of hope has for them. "May the God of hope fill you with all joy and peace as you trust in him, so that you may overflow with hope by the power of the Holy Spirit" (Rom. 15:13).

Hope therefore engenders a well-being that is based on one's relation with God, not on things around. Job warns of false trust: "If I have put my trust in gold or said to pure gold, 'You are my security,' . . . then these also would be sins to be judged, for I would have been unfaithful to God on high" (Job 31:24, 28).

Now see what hope produces in us:

1. *Endurance.* Paul writes of "endurance inspired by hope in our Lord Jesus Christ" (1 Thess. 1:3). Then he tells the Roman believers, "We know that suffering produces perseverance; perseverance, character; and character, hope" (Rom. 5:3-4). Notice the cycle: hope inspires endurance, and ultimately from perseverance, hope rises in strengthened character.

2. *Purity.* The apostle John admits that much of our future glory is hidden from us. But "when he appears, we shall be like him, for we shall see him as he is. Everyone who has this hope in him purifies himself, just as he is pure" (1 John 3:2-3).

3. *Encouragement.* The Christian's hope of rising, even from death, to meet the Lord in the air and then being with him forever stirs Paul to prompt believers to "encourage each other with these words" (1 Thess. 4:18).

Thoughtful reflection on the subject of hope will make it

immediately apparent that any expectation involves the future. "Hope that is seen is no hope at all. Who hopes for what he already has? But if we hope for what we do not yet have, we wait for it patiently" (Rom. 8:24-25).

Such hope must be sustained because it tends to wilt amid the blighting influences of our present life. Here is the means for this sustenance, given by God: "Everything that was written in the past was written to teach us, so that through endurance and the encouragement of the Scriptures we might have hope" (Rom. 15:4). "Therefore we do not lose heart. Though outwardly we are wasting away, yet inwardly we are being renewed day by day. For our light and momentary troubles are achieving for us an eternal glory that far outweighs them all. So we fix our eyes not on what is seen, but on what is unseen. For what is seen is temporary, but what is unseen is eternal" (2 Cor. 4:16-18).

Nor is this tenaciousness self-generated; it too is of God. "Now the Lord is the Spirit, and where the Spirit of the Lord is, there is freedom. And we, who with unveiled faces all reflect the Lord's glory, are being transformed into his likeness with ever-increasing glory, which comes from the Lord, who is the Spirit" (2 Cor. 3:17-18).

Looking through the lens of Scripture, we see our future home and hear our Father's voice: "You will receive a rich welcome into the eternal kingdom of our Lord and Savior Jesus Christ" (2 Peter 1:11). And, "They will sparkle in his land like jewels in a crown. How attractive and beautiful they will be!" (Zech. 9:16-17).

# APPENDIX 5

## WHY DO FORGIVEN PEOPLE STILL DIE?

Here is a question asked by Christians throughout the ages: If death is the punishment for sin, then why do the righteous, whose sins are forgiven, still die?

Remember, first of all, our definition of death. The punishment of death fell on Adam the moment he sinned. He lost right standing with God, and being thus guilty, he was sentenced to death, just as he had been warned. First, he died in his inner person and became depraved in character. Next, he and Eve were driven from the Garden of Eden.

This expulsion cost them more than flowers and real estate. They lost their intimate fellowship with God. As God's life-giving Spirit was withdrawn, the corrupting infection of sin seized them, ultimately dragging them, and all their descendants, into the grave.

This sad story, however, has a happy ending for those who believe in Jesus Christ, whose very name and messianic title point to him as our Savior from sin and its penalty and the One who restores to us the Spirit of God. Physical death might still come, but the element of punishment is removed.

Consider the following illustration. Several of my children, in their teens, worked at a nearby carbon factory. Each day they returned home with black carbon dust covering them and their clothes. Wherever they stepped or touched, a black grime marked their trail. My wife made a firm decision: no carbon worker could enter our home without first passing through our outside building, located only a few steps from our back door. There, all their clothes could be deposited in a tub, a special covering robe was put on, and they headed directly to the shower. Clean and refreshed, they came to the table.

In mercy, God passes us through the outside building, or grave, where we shed our carbon covering and are made ready for his table. God is not punishing his children. The punitive element was removed on Calvary's cross. Look deeply at these words:

> I declare to you, brothers, that flesh and blood cannot inherit the kingdom of God, nor does the perishable inherit the imperishable. Listen, I tell you a mystery: We will not all sleep, but we will all be changed—in a flash, in the twinkling of an eye, at the last trumpet. For the trumpet will sound, the dead will be raised imperishable, and we will be changed. For the perishable must clothe itself with the imperishable, and the mortal with immortality. When the perishable has been clothed with the imperishable, and the mortal with immortality, then the saying that is written will come true: "Death has been swallowed up in victory."
> "Where, O death, is your victory?
> Where, O death, is your sting?"
> The sting of death is sin, and the power of sin is the law. But thanks be to God! He gives us the victory through our Lord Jesus Christ. (1 Cor. 15:50-57)

Our hearts can be lifted and understanding enlightened by this Scripture if we distinguish God's two methods of shielding his home and removing from us our carbon-covered clothing.

250

Everyone passes through the outside building of the grave, except for the final generation, who are met and changed outside the door, in an instant, by our Lord's power. Whether we go through the outside building or not, God is dealing in love and mercy with his children. They never perish. Eternal death is not their lot. This assurance underlies Jesus' very precious promise: "I am the resurrection and the life. He who believes in me will live, even though he dies; and whoever lives and believes in me will never die" (John 11:25-26).

# Appendix 6

## Truncated Truth Disease

### (Take this test to see if you are infected!)

Sad but true, overfamiliarity can hide the powerful meaning of Bible texts and thus hide Jesus from us. Gospel preachers faithfully warn sinners to turn to the Savior, using Scripture to point them to the cross, but in their rush to get across the saving message, the context is often lost from many an atonement passage.

Rather than arguing the point, permit me to give you a simple test. I urge you, thoughtful reader, to take a sheet of paper and jot down your answers to the following eight questions. (First, though, make sure you hide the answers!) Perhaps you will learn something surprising about yourself.

Below is a list of often-used, very precious atonement texts, along with questions to be answered—with your Bible closed for now, please. I am seeking to make the point that all too many of us read and repeatedly proclaim Scriptures without using them as they are given, in their immediate setting.

### Questions

1. "Even death on a cross." As used in their setting, what are these words aimed at?
2. "The Son of Man . . . [came] to give his life as a ransom for

many." What occasioned this important teaching? What is Jesus aiming at here?

3. Jesus "gave himself for our sins to rescue us from _____." Complete the sentence.

4. "You were redeemed from _____ with the precious blood of Christ, a lamb without blemish or defect." Fill in the blank.

5. "He himself bore our sins in his body on the tree, so that we might die to sins and live for righteousness; by his wounds you have been healed." In its context, what is the immediate purpose of this powerful atonement text?

6. "Christ died for sins once for all, the righteous for the unrighteous, to bring you to God." On the basis of the verses preceding this much-loved text, what point is it making?

7. Jesus Christ "gave himself for us to redeem us from _____ and to _____." Fill in the blanks.

8. "All have sinned and fall short of the glory of God, and _____." Complete the sentence.

## Answers

1. The quote is from Philippians 2:8. The apostle aims to show that Jesus' death on the cross for our sins was, at the same time, the most powerful antidote to selfish living. Notice that the context for this teaching involves the entire chapter. In other words, the Bible's extended teaching on Christ's incarnation and sacrifice is here used as the supreme example of godly submission—along with the examples of Timothy and Epaphroditus.

2. Christ speaks of giving his life as a ransom for us sinners in Matthew 20:28, also in Mark 10:45, in order to quell the jealous uprising among his disciples. Notice what precedes

these texts.

3. "Who gave himself for our sins to rescue us from **the present evil age**" (Gal. 1:4).

4. "You were redeemed from **the empty way of life handed down to you from your forefathers**"; it was "with the precious blood of Christ, a lamb without blemish or defect" (1 Peter 1:18-19).

5. This verse—1 Peter 2:24—clearly sets forth a supreme example in godly submission. See the word "submit" in verse 13 and again in 18, leading into, "To this were you called, because Christ suffered for you, leaving you an example, that you should follow in his steps" (v. 21). These words lead into our text verse 24 and rather directly take us into instructions for wives and husbands. The wife is to be submissive, and the husband is forbidden to be controlling but, instead, must be considerate and responsible for her well-being.

6. The words that lead into "Christ died for sins" (1 Peter 3:18) are these: "keeping a clear conscience, so that those who speak maliciously against your good behavior in Christ may be ashamed of their slander. It is better, if it is God's will, to suffer for doing good than for doing evil" (vv. 16-17).

7. Jesus Christ "gave himself for us to redeem us from all wickedness and to purify for himself a people that are his very own, eager to do what is good" (Titus 2:14). The apostle adds, "These, then, are the things you should teach" (v. 15).

8. "All have sinned and fall short of the glory of God, and are justified freely by his grace through the redemption that came by Christ Jesus" (Rom. 3:23-24). The idea of the sentence is not simply to convince us that sin is universal but to make clear that sinners may have justification through Christ's gracious redemption.

## What Are We to Make of This?

If the above Scriptures are used today almost solely as proof texts to proclaim the atonement, we must ask, Why are the apostles' own points of teaching so rarely presented? I am not saying that it is wrong to expound salvation truth supported by these texts. But why are the objectives of the inspired writers so lost?

If my supposition is correct that the majority of those taking the test score rather poorly, then I must again press the question, Why? It is undoubtedly because, in each case, the great lessons of the larger text have been consciously or unconsciously discarded. When we fail to let the cross go beyond the way to heaven, we do great injury. Salvation that cost our Lord's death for us demands our life for him: "He died for all, that those who live should no longer live for themselves but for him who died for them and was raised again" (2 Cor. 5:15). The freedom given by grace is from sin and unto godliness. All too often this truth has become a casualty of the truncated teaching all around us.

How sad it is that the church, which has weathered the onslaughts of higher criticism, modern secularism, and encroaching mysticism, is now having its legs cut from under it by incomplete, stunted preaching and teaching!

# APPENDIX 7

## HELPING THE VERY YOUNG CHILD TO UNDERSTAND SIN AND DEATH

Following is a letter I wrote to parents of a young daughter about seven years old whose newborn baby brother died, leaving her in inner turmoil.

> Dear —— [Mother and Father],
>
> You are in our prayers these days. I pray that you will know his beyond-all-explaining peace (Phil. 4:4-7) and that this letter will help in directing C—— into the Lord's rest.
>
> First of all, her recent questions stem from her sense of loss and the confusion of emotions, concern for parents and their grief, personal sorrow, and even a ruffled selfishness (which underlies much of adult grief because we are sinners). It is doubly hard for a child when heavier losses come before matured ability to identify and handle the pangs.
>
> A basic axiom to keep in mind is this: all children can ask questions which require answers that are beyond their capacity to receive and understand. (Maybe reread this!) C—— is very bright and very sensitive. This makes it more difficult—but not at all impossible.
>
> Therefore, you might begin at this point: "C——, will you one day discipline your children? Will they *always*

understand and like all that you do when you must punish or deny certain things? Right! And sometimes they will not know how much you love them and will only think of the things that give them pain. But all the while you will love them and keep working hard for their good. It's the same way with the Father in heaven. We are his children, and we don't always understand things, especially when we are hurt. But then we study the cross and know how much he loves us. All that suffering Jesus went through really troubled Jesus' disciples. Then everyone was surprised because it brought forth so much good! Our sufferings and sorrows came into the world through our sin, and we all suffer—but God in love keeps bringing blessings to us.

"Adam is the daddy of all the human family. We get our name, reputation, character, and material things from our fathers. When a father turns to sin—like Adam, and also Eve, did—it hurts the whole family.

"But then Jesus takes over as head of the Christian family, and we get salvation riches and blessing from him. All this is taught in 1 Corinthians 15:21-22. We are now in God's special family. We cannot simply blame Adam and Eve. We also sin—even after we know all this. Now, when little ones go to be with Jesus, they are taken away from all evil and go into the Lord's presence without ever doing any wrong. If they had lived a few years longer, they would have sinned like we all do because of our bad hearts. But, you see, God kept them from the bad experiences of sin.

"None of us fully understands all this, and these sufferings hurt a lot, but we must simply *trust* God. We love him and know he never does wrong." Study 1 Corinthians 13:12.

Well, —— [Mom and Dad], I hope this helps. You dare not overmagnify the matter, and yet it must not be ignored either. God give you balance and confidence.

Your friend in Christ,
Pastor Burchett

# INDEX OF SCRIPTURES CITED

www.ingramcontent.com/pod-product-compliance
Lightning Source LLC
Chambersburg PA
CBHW060229050426
42448CB00009B/1362